"I am genuinely grateful to Tim Sinclair for writing this book. He put into words what I have often felt, but have been unable to articulate. As I read it, I kept finding myself quietly agreeing with it under my breath. Well-researched, well thought-out, and well-written, *Branded* has given this generation of Christ-followers not just something to think about, but something to do. When I finished reading the book, I handed it to my wife and encouraged her to read it too. Way to go, Tim."—**Dr. Will Davis Jr**, Sr. Pastor, Austin Christian Fellowship, author of *Pray Big*

"Tim Sinclair's *Branded* is an honest attempt to plant the needed seeds of change in the hearts of Christians to help better share the beauty of Christ. Sinclair reminds us that Christ is perfect, and there is no need to force, embellish, or hide the story of our walk with Him. Convicting at times and outright hilarious at others, *Branded* is, at its heart, a simple plea for all of us to be true to the artists God created us to be. In Sinclair's words, 'If you're open, honest, real, and raw—millions of people will resonate with your story anyway, flaws and all.' *Branded* is the perfect pep talk you need to truly share Christ with a consumer culture."—**Dave Frey**, lead singer of Sidewalk Prophets

"Communicating the authentic Christ in a high-tech, consumer-oriented, and distracted environment is a challenge—at least if you're concerned about doing it effectively. Tim Sinclair has done us a huge favor by unwrapping the mind-set of our culture and enabling us to take the message of Jesus into it relevantly yet without compromise. Anyone who is interested in representing Jesus well in our day needs to read this book."—**Joe Stowell**, President, Cornerstone University

"There's a reason why Tim Sinclair is successful in Christian radio: He's a top-flight communicator, period. Here's hoping we all have a growing passion, like Tim, to communicate Christ as clearly as we can."—**Brant Hanson**, Syndicated Radio Host, *Mornings with Brant*

"A great book for all of us involved in sharing the joy of Jesus. Tim offers a great perspective, in easy-to-understand terms, with a unique sense of humor."—**Alan Mason**, Chief Operating Officer, K-LOVE & Air 1

BRANDED

SHARING JESUS WITH A CONSUMER CULTURE

TIM SINCLAIR

Kregel
Publications

Branded: Sharing Jesus with a Consumer Culture
© 2011 by Tim Sinclair

Published by Kregel Publications, a division of Kregel, Inc.,
P.O. Box 2607, Grand Rapids, MI 49501.

Library of Congress Cataloging-in-Publication Data
Sinclair, Tim
   Branded : sharing Jesus with a consumer culture / Tim
Sinclair.
      p. cm.
   1. Witness bearing (Christianity) 2. Consumption (Economics)
—Religious aspects—Christianity. I. Title.
BV4520.S465   2011   248'.5—dc22   2011002362

ISBN 978-0-8254-3894-3

Printed in the United States of America

11 12 13 14 15 / 5 4 3 2 1

*For Jeremiah and
Elijah—
More than anyone else
in the world,
it's you guys I hope to
share Jesus with*

Contents

Preface

Having spent the majority of my career writing, voicing, and producing radio advertisements, I've found beauty in the minimalism of the process. In the industry we call it "theater of the mind." Essentially, radio provides the basics (or the backdrop) and allows you, the listener, to fill in the gaps with your own imagination, experience, and value system. Radio writes the script, and lets *you* be the director, the producer, the makeup artist, and the choreographer.

For example, let's say it's Christmastime. You're in the car on the way to work when your favorite radio station airs a spot for Kay Jewelers. As quiet carols play in the background, you hear someone tearing wrapping paper, gently opening a small box, and then gasping at the sight of what's inside. The announcer softly says, "This Christmas, every kiss begins with Kay."

During those thirty seconds, what did you picture? How many people were involved in the scene? Were they in a house or an apartment? Were they white or black? Was it daytime or nighttime? Was their Christmas tree decorated with colored lights or white lights? Was the package wrapped in beautiful paper or in the Sunday comics? Was there a diamond ring or a pearl necklace in the box?

Chances are, you imagined the situation exactly as if it were happening to *you*. If you are a part of a white family of four, living in an apartment, who generally celebrates Christmas first thing in the morning under an artificial tree with colored lights, that's what you pictured. If your surroundings are dramatically different, your mind likely created those pictures instead. Radio provides the basics and lets *you* adapt the rest to fit your specific situation. Pretty cool, isn't it?

If this very same commercial were on television, a casting director would have made all those decisions for you. He or she would have also selected the style of furniture, the pictures on the wall, the music coming from the stereo, and the actors' clothing. That's all fine, but it leaves no room for looking through your own lens. No room for inserting your own life and style into the drama.

This book was written like a radio advertisement.

I'm convinced that when it comes to showing and sharing Jesus to and with the world around us, it's critical that we recognize our own unique situations, talents, abilities—and then effectively use them to reach people within our individual spheres of influence. Other than the boundaries and guidelines provided by the Bible, nothing else should create a game plan for us because there is no right way for everybody. There is no one-size-fits-all methodology.

So I'm not going to give you one.

I'll set the backdrop, and let you take it from there.

Introduction

Pretending or Living?

"It's weird. I'm a Christian, and even I don't like us very much."

I can't tell you how many people have said something like that to me over the years. I have to admit I've had the same thought at times. Maybe you have as well. Perhaps it came when the church you once thought was safe turned out to be full of judgmental cliques. Or when the small group Bible study you used to attend turned out to be a bunch of gossipy socialites. Or after the guys you saw pray around the conference table at lunch turned out to be the ones who chased women and drank too much on business trips.

Call it hypocrisy, call it insincerity, call it whatever you want. The bottom line is that many Christians have an "-ing" problem. We're pretty good at say-*ing*, but not so good at do-*ing*. We're pretty good at act-*ing*, but not so good at be-*ing*. We're pretty good at pretend-*ing*, but not so good at truly liv-*ing*.

I don't know about you, but it seems that to compensate for that deficit (and make ourselves feel better), those of us who are Christians have attempted to "brand" our relationship with Jesus. Rather than actually trying to change, we've instead decided to make the world *think* that we're different. *Think* that we're holy. *Think* that we're transformed. We've covered ourselves up with all sorts of meaningless trinkets and rituals that (in our own heads) permit us to *show* one thing, yet *be* another.

We put "Jesus Saves" bumper stickers on our cars so we don't feel as bad about driving eighty miles per hour on the interstate. We listen to Christian radio during our morning commutes so we don't feel as bad about watching *Desperate Housewives* the night before. We post uplifting, churchy things on our Facebook pages so we don't feel as bad about routinely belittling our kids. You get the idea.

Fortunately or unfortunately, the world is watching, and our ridiculous actions aren't fooling anyone. Those who don't know Christ aren't buying the act. In fact, they're ignoring it. Following Jesus has become to them like a high school variety show, complete with dated costumes, cheesy songs, and bad acting.

I think it's time to change that perception.

Your impact (and mine) on our friends, family, and co-workers has nothing to do with the sayings on our bumpers or the symbols around our necks. It has nothing to do with the number of Bible verses we tweet or the biblical names we give our kids. It has nothing to do with how many times we go to church or how often we put money in the offering plate.

Rather, sharing Jesus with today's culture has *everything* to do with being personally *branded* by Christ. With being forever changed by Jesus. With being permanently marked by our Savior. I *can't* promise you the process won't hurt a little, but I *can* promise you that it will be well worth it.

1 Caught Off Guard

Why Branded *Was Written*

If you've been sucked into the worlds of Facebook and Twitter like I have, you know these social networking websites are good for two things:

1. Reuniting with family, professional contacts, and old friends.
2. Wasting excessive amounts of time.

Personally, I've done plenty of both.

I've connected with hundreds of people I knew from grade school. I've kept in touch with relatives who live in other parts of the country. I've learned that I'm most like Chandler from *Friends* and that if I were a state, I'd be Wyoming.

Apparently, I'm square and boring too.

A few months ago, I received a startling Facebook message from an old high school friend. He and I weren't particularly close, but we played quite a bit of basketball together. I'll call him Alan.

Alan had quietly been following my status updates and blog. Seeing that I was fairly verbal about my Christian faith, Alan said that he too was compelled to share his personal belief system with me.

Talk about being caught off guard.

As a follower of Christ, wasn't it *me* who was supposed to be sharing my faith with *him*? Wasn't *I* the one who was supposed to be seeking out people who didn't share my beliefs? Wasn't *my* message the one commonly called "the greatest story ever told"?

In a lengthy collection of paragraphs, Alan shared that in the years following our time in high school he had become an agnostic. He explained that he just couldn't bring himself to believe in an entity "of which there is no evidence."

> Just as you can not disprove a monster I claim to have seen, I can not disprove a god in which you believe . . . I feel you have more to learn from somebody like me than from a mindless follower who follows the Christian faith simply because they were brought up in it and never really thought about it.

Maybe so.

If I hadn't realized it already, I realized it after that message from Alan. Christianity's monopoly of the "faith marketplace" has slipped away. Sadly, most Christians haven't noticed. Many don't even seem to care.

It used to be that people believed something to be true because the Bible said it was.

It used to be that spirituality was synonymous with Christianity.

It used to be.

Alan is the perfect example of this cultural shift. He wrote it this way:

> I was raised attending church, but I remember independently thinking religion was hogwash very early in life. I just wonder

if you've ever really wondered why you believe it [the Bible] as literal? I don't think we choose to believe, I think we just believe. But at some point we reevaluate and really think for ourselves.

He isn't alone in his sentiments. Not by a long shot.

Unlike a generation or two ago, these days the Christian faith has significant competition. Lots of it. Kabbalah, Scientology, Islam, Buddhism, Hinduism. Even atheists and agnostics (like Alan) have faith, though it's in the idea that either there is no God or that He can't be proven.

It seems many Christians wish this type of spiritual competition would suddenly go away. They wish life could go back to how it used to be—when people believed in the God of the Bible "just because." They wish they didn't have to engage in difficult conversations with people like Alan who ask hard questions.

If you are one of these people, let me warn you: this book is *full* of hard questions. And ironically it's not full of answers—at least not specific ones. If you're looking for an evangelism instruction manual or a how-to check-list, you'll want to set this book down and find something else.

I'm convinced that checklists are a part of the problem—not the solution. For years Christians have blindly (yet with good intentions) stuck their heads in evangelism playbooks, ignoring what was going on around them. We pretended there was a one-two-three process for leading a friend to Jesus—or a recipe for converting your co-workers. Maybe there was one at some point. Maybe. But there's certainly not one anymore.

Branded, by design, is a pep talk, not a playbook. It's motivation, not mechanics. It's inspiration, not instruction. It's the start of a very long, perhaps never-ending, discussion that's desperately needed.

2 Putting Lipstick on a Pig

What Branding Jesus Is (and Isn't)

Evangelism = Marketing Jesus

If you're feeling a little twitchy now, don't be alarmed. It's completely natural. Many people find themselves uncomfortable when they see the words *Jesus* and *marketing* in the same sentence. They think, *Jesus isn't a product, He's a person. Christianity isn't a futon, it's a faith. We can't sell them like they are . . . right?*

You be the judge.

Merriam-Webster defines the word *marketing* as "the process or technique of promoting, selling, and distributing a product or service." Personally, I would define *evangelism* pretty much the same way. Evangelism is the process or technique of promoting, selling, and distributing Jesus. The Bible lays it out this way: "[Jesus] said to them, 'Go into all the world and preach the gospel to all creation'" (Mark 16:15 NIV).

From those words, it's clear that those of us who know Christ have been called to show (promote), share (sell), and spread (distribute) Him. Fighting or fretting over whether the process should be called "evangelism" or "marketing" or "branding" is just semantics.

The Morality of Marketing

My wife and I had a "discussion" one night about the ethics of marketing. (For you single folks, "discussion" is married-person speak for "argument.")

During another chaotic dinner with our newborn and two-year-old, my lovely bride explained to me that marketing (in general) is a con game. It's one person or entity trying to trick another person or entity into buying something they don't want or need. It's dressing up something ugly with something pretty to get a sale. It's embellishment. It's hype. It's lying. It's putting lipstick on a pig.

Since branding various businesses, products, causes, and ideas is a large part of my job (and the focus of this book), I took offense at her perception. (Thus, our "discussion.") Was she calling me a liar? Was she ashamed of what I did for a living? Would she make me sleep on the couch if I pointed out that I "marketed" myself to her while we were dating?

Since I value my well-worn spot in our bed, my explanation to her was simple and without mention of our courtship. I basically said that people are *going* to buy stuff. They have to. And when they do, they might as well buy *my* stuff. Or my client's stuff. And when it comes to faith, if they're going to choose, they might as well choose my Jesus.

As we talked, it became obvious that my wife's issue wasn't really with *marketing*, per se. Her problem was with the perceived motivation of many *marketers*. (Again, if you're single, married people often spend hours "discussing" things that aren't the actual causes of contention.) In a nutshell, she felt like most people trying to sell her something were actually trying to take advantage of her.

It's easy to see why.

Infomercials frequently prey on people's late-night impulses by selling mediocre products in bulk and adding exorbitant processing or handling charges to the bill. Mechanics often take advantage of clients who don't know any better by "fixing" things that aren't broken. Some dentists do the same. Salesmen point people to the products that pay the highest commission by focusing on their own wallets, rather than the customers' needs.

Do these examples mean all marketers are evil? Of course not. But they do indicate that, for people "selling Jesus," the groundwork has already been laid for Christians to fail. We're perceived to be selling something, which ensures that our motivations will automatically be questioned (and likely challenged).

Much of the world—including many of your friends, family, and co-workers—thinks that Christians are nothing more than pitchmen shouting about the latest product that must be bought *right now*. We're the greasy-fingered guys at the garage trying to sell them a radiator they don't need. We're the slick used-car salesmen attempting to smooth-talk our way into a deal that they're going to regret.

We're marketers hawking yet another product that they don't want.

As our discussion (and our dinner) wound to a close, my wife and I came to the same conclusion about marketing. Whether you're endorsing a Jeep or a jacket or Jesus, money, power, fame, and prestige are the *wrong* motivators. Obligation and desperation aren't very good ones either. Each is self-centered and probably dishonest, and most potential buyers can see those things a mile away.

We agreed that there is only one *right* motivation to sell something—belief.

Belief that your product is the best.

Belief that the up-front costs are worth the long-term benefit.

Belief that your service will make a lasting difference in someone's life.

(As an aside, belief doesn't necessarily make you *right*, but it does make you *authentic*, and that's a huge step in the right direction.)

As a radio personality, I have a rule. I will never ask my listeners to do something I'm not willing to do myself. If I don't believe enough in the importance of giving blood or donating to Haiti or financially supporting our nonprofit radio ministry, then I'm not going to be effective in asking anyone else to do so.

Mathematically stated: Branding − Believing = Baloney.

When it comes to branding *Jesus*, it's safe to assume that belief is at least a small part of every Christian's motivation equation. But be honest, how often do you find yourself letting other factors get in the way: obligation, power, prestige? Have you ever been tempted to try to fulfill some sort of conversion quota? Have you ever looked forward to telling everyone at church about your salvation success? Have you ever imagined how wonderful it would be to become the person others approach to learn about effective evangelism?

Maybe it's just me, but I think that sometimes Christ-followers get so focused on our own selfish goals, we can't tell the difference between lying people to Jesus and leading people to Jesus. Between conning them and convincing them. Between manipulating and marketing.

Before you or I can hope to effectively sell anything (especially our Savior), our motivation has to be pure. We must set aside every selfish thought and every impure motive—then live out what we believe as best we know how. Anything less is self-serving and, dare I say, sinful.

Mission vs. Tactics

Just as marketing Jesus doesn't imply that we con people into a relationship with Him, it also doesn't imply that we change what Christians believe or what the Bible says. There's a fear among many in the church, and understandably so, that adjusting our evangelism methods will lead to softening our values. To condoning sin in an effort to draw crowds. To "widening the gate" to attract a newer (and larger) subset of people. That's not the case at all. Branding Jesus is not a change in mission—it's a change in tactics.

By my definition, "mission" is who you are called to be and what you are called to do—regardless of time, situation, or cultural change. "Tactics" are the methods by which you try to achieve your mission . . . taking into account those three variables.

Missions don't change. Tactics do (or should).

In the corporate world, look at Movie Gallery and Waldenbooks. Each company was clearly committed to its respective mission of renting videos or selling books. But each company was also committed to its tactics. Too committed.

Movie Gallery refused to acknowledge (in time) that online rentals, on-demand video, and vending machine–style rental outlets were more efficient and more effective tactics for renting movies. Netflix, Comcast, and RedBox each shared the same mission as Movie Gallery, but their updated delivery processes and incredibly low prices vaulted them light-years ahead of traditional video rental stores.

Waldenbooks, now owned by Borders, failed to recognize that book buyers demand more than just semiconvenient mall locations. They need a great price and/or a relaxing atmosphere, complete with chairs, coffee, music, and wi-fi. Amazon.com and Barnes & Noble figured it out. One created a zero-overhead, low-price online store, while the other created a comfortable, casual, contemporary bookstore that doubled as a coffee shop and wireless hot spot.

While RedBox and Barnes & Noble were creating new strategies for their industries, Movie Gallery was forced to file for Chapter 11 bankruptcy in

2007. On April 30, 2010, the company announced it would be closing and liquidating all of its stores after filing for Chapter 7. Waldenbooks shuttered more than five hundred locations between 2001 and 2008, while its remaining stores have been converted to the "Borders Express" brand.

Same mission. Different tactics. Very different results.

The mission versus tactics issue can get a little sticky, however, when it comes to faith. Our mission as Christians is clear: Make disciples. Find people willing to put their faith and trust in Jesus. (Again, Mark 16:15 spells that out for us.) It's just that the means by which we *fulfill* that mission has caused many believers to get their choir robes in a bunch.

Our tendency is to "do things the way they've always been done," often assuming those things are biblical, as opposed to just traditional. But the Bible gives no specific instructions as to the methods with which we share our faith. We're just told to, and I know I'm paraphrasing, "get 'er done."

It was a human, not Jesus, who created "The Four Spiritual Laws" tract. It was a human, not Jesus, who wrote "I Have Decided to Follow Jesus." It was a human, not Jesus, who put together the little flip book with all of the colors. It was a human, not Jesus, who first scribbled out that "cross bridging the chasm" drawing. It's not that any of these things are wrong, it's just that they're not necessarily as effective anymore. And that's okay. Really.

Here's what we *do* know. Jesus had the remarkable ability to be culturally and socially relevant, while still delivering a powerful, life-changing message. Two thousand years ago, Jesus spoke of shepherds and sheep, vineyards and fields, sowing and reaping. He used things like olives, wine, fish, and mustard seeds in His analogies. Each item was ingrained in the fabric of the first century. The people He was sharing with *instantly* related to the stories.

If Jesus were to walk the earth today, I can't help but think He'd be discussing *Lost* instead of "The Lost Sheep" or Pearl Jam instead of "The Pearl of Great Price." His stories would likely center around iPods, movies, coffee, and the stock market. Yet somehow there are twenty-first-century Christians who still feel the need to talk to unbelievers about "the wheat and the chaff" or "the vine and the branches." (For the record, I think each of these would be a fabulous name for a Christian a capella group. Thank me later.)

Our mission is the same as it was during Jesus' day, but the time, situation, and cultural expectations are not. As Movie Gallery and Waldenbooks discovered in the corporate world, remaining too committed to our tactics (as Christians) will lead our culture into spiritual bankruptcy and moral decline. In many ways, I believe it already has.

Painting with a Broad Brush

Pat Robertson has done many positive things, but it seems to me he has recently been guilty of being too committed to his own tactics. I call his strategy the "shock and awe" approach—which boils down to making over-the-top statements with the purpose of riling up the media and those who religiously follow it. It's the any-publicity-is-good-publicity theory.

You no doubt heard about *The 700 Club* host's untimely comments shortly after the devastating 2010 earthquake in Haiti. Days after a massive tremor struck Port-au-Prince, killing hundreds of thousands of innocent people, Robertson said (in effect) that God was punishing the people of Haiti for making a "pact to the devil."

Though there were shreds of truth in it, that statement didn't go over well. At all. Every mainstream news channel, newspaper, and magazine lashed out at Robertson (and often Christians in general) for such a heartless view of such a tragedy.

> "It never ceases to amaze that in times of amazing human suffering somebody says something that could be so utterly stupid." —White House Press Secretary Robert Gibbs

"It is shameful for anyone—but especially a so-called minister of the gospel—to suggest that God or the poor people of Haiti had anything to do with it." —David Waters, former editor of the *Washington Post* "On Faith" column

"Go to Hell, Pat Robertson—and the sooner the better. Your 'theological' nonsense is revolting . . . Haiti is suffering a catastrophe and you offer silliness at best, and racism at the worst." —Rev. Paul Raushenbush, religion editor for the *Huffington Post*

As I listened to these comments (and hundreds like them), I was frustrated. Annoyed even. Though not for the reasons you might think.

I wasn't frustrated by Mr. Robertson himself. He has said similar things before (like after Hurricane Katrina) and he'll likely say them again. At this point, I pretty much expect them.

I wasn't even frustrated by what he said. Everyone is entitled to his or her own opinions, no matter how off-the-wall. I'm sure I have a few of them myself.

I was frustrated that, because of Mr. Robertson's visibility, he painted *all* Christians as unloving, uncaring extremists. And he did it with a really big brush.

Whether we like it or not, the world makes assumptions about you and me based on what they see in the media. The archaic *tactics* of high-profile believers make our day-to-day job of sharing Jesus increasingly difficult. And frankly, that stinks. We've got little watercolor brushes, while Pat Robertson and other Christian "lightning rods" have nine-inch power rollers. Their "spray" has (in many cases) tainted the view of millions . . . many of whom you and I are trying to reach.

Though it's frustrating, here's how I've come to think about these situations: The one thing tiny brushes *can* do that big ones *can't* is get close to things.

Have you ever tried cutting in around crown molding with a gigantic, bristly monstrosity? It's next to impossible. You need a narrow, pointed brush. It requires time. It requires effort. But the results can be breathtaking.

The same is true as you and I attempt to re-market Jesus in this media-crazy culture. While the Pat Robertsons spray from afar, the rest of us can get up close and personal with people. Instead of offering a ten-second video clip on YouTube, we can spend hours getting to know people in person. Instead of throwing out a flippant sound bite on NPR, we can do the hard (but worthwhile) work of truly investing in someone's life, one-on-one.

By implementing loving, open-arms tactics, we can paint a much more detailed (and much more accurate) picture of what our Jesus is really all about.

3 Playing Monopoly by Yourself

What Branding Jesus Is Up Against

The Religious Marketplace

Spend any time in the business world, and you'll discover that Monopoly is more than just a game that families play when the electricity goes out. It's real life.

No matter how big or small, most companies on the planet want to dominate their respective marketplace. Given the choice, each would gladly clear the playing field and become the only option for a specific product or service.

It would make life easy. Wouldn't it?

Maybe temporarily, but a total monopoly wouldn't make life any better.

Lack of competition breeds laziness. Laziness breeds apathy. And eventually, apathy breeds disaster.

Absent of competition, CEOs don't watch the bottom line as closely. Designers don't create innovative products as regularly. Marketers don't try to spread the word as effectively. Salespeople don't learn to showcase the benefits of their product as creatively. And worst of all, customers don't feel passion for the brand as frequently.

The dirty little secret in marketing is that without passionate customers, brands die. Sometimes it takes months, years, or decades. But in the end, dead is still dead. The time it takes for a company to whither away is irrelevant.

Coke wouldn't taste as good without Pepsi. Toyotas wouldn't drive as smoothly without Hondas. Google wouldn't search as efficiently without Yahoo! McDonald's wouldn't taste as good without Burger King. Dave wouldn't be as funny without Jay.

"So what?"

"I don't run a business."

"This doesn't apply to me."

Actually, as a person of faith, it does.

For years in America, Christianity held a monopoly in the so-called "religious marketplace." Either you went to First Baptist or you didn't go to church at all. You sang three hymns, passed the plate, and listened to a thirty-minute message—or you slept in, mowed the lawn, and watched football. You showered, put on a suit and tie, and drove to church—or you grabbed a hat, threw on sweatpants, and drove to the gas station for a newspaper and a doughnut.

There were very few options. Christians knew it. And we got lazy. Then we became apathetic. We have slowly transformed into a passionless people, and now our brand is dying.

Like Sand Through the Hourglass

While we're talking about board games, I assume you're familiar with the tiny plastic timers that come with many of them. These timers are often yellow on the top and bottom, transparent in the middle, and have tiny white grains of something on the inside. (I thought it might be sugar, but it's not.

Don't ask me how I know.) For decades, these simple devices have helped game players keep track of time.

As the glass is placed on one of its feet, the white granules slowly make their way from the top section to the bottom—usually taking a minute or two. Once the top of the timer is empty and the bottom is full, everything stops. The game. The sand. Everything. To resume play, the timer has to be flipped over.

For me, *Branded* is a call to turn the Christian hourglass over. It's an acknowledgment that most of the sand is sitting uselessly at the bottom, and if we hope to see new movement or progress, we need to make drastic changes. We might even have to stand on our heads for a while.

Branding Jesus (and becoming branded by Him ourselves) will require rethinking the way evangelism has always been done. It will require challenging the status quo. It will require questioning the effectiveness of our current methods. It will require regaining our passion, reenergizing our base, and rebuilding our personal outreach strategies from the ground up.

I Was Told There'd Be No Math

I suppose it's natural to first ask whether Jesus *needs* to be re-branded or re-marketed. Yes, we have a more fragmented, diversified culture. Yes, we see more religious options out there. But isn't Jesus still the market leader? Aren't Christians being as effective as they've always been? Hasn't there been consistency in the number of people who are embracing Christ over the years?

Well, I'm not a numbers guy, and (trust me) this isn't a numbers book. But there are a few left-brained concepts (aka "actual studies") that I think will be helpful in finding the answers.

The first piece of data that I recently uncovered was this: According to the *World Christian Encyclopedia*, the church spends $1,551,466 for each new follower of Jesus.

Let that sink in for a second.

That means if your church's annual budget is $500,000, it would (on average) bring one person to Christ every three years! Seeing that kind of ratio on a balance sheet would get every CEO in America fired. And it should. Though there are *many* churches that are effective at outreach, as a whole, it appears as if all the money we pour into our pastors, programs, pageants, and PowerPoint presentations isn't effective. It's not exciting the people *inside* the church enough to go reach people *outside* the church.

We've seemingly created places of worship that *keep* people in . . . but don't *bring* people in. Or send passion-filled people out. If the *World Christian Encyclopedia* figures are correct, today's Christians have essentially run some really expensive bathwater, sat down, and gotten all wrinkly from stewing in our own, pricey filth.

In 2007, a group of people at the Pew Forum on Religion and Public Life (who are all much smarter than me) released some other very telling figures. Here's what their studies found:

- Barely half of all Americans call themselves Protestant (51.3 percent).

By the time you read this, all evidence suggests that Protestants will no longer be the majority in the United States. For reference, about two-thirds of Americans called themselves Protestant in the 1980s. With that kind of decline every year, Protestants will effectively be gone within our lifetime.

- More than one-quarter of people have left the faith in which they were raised (28 percent).

As you'll see later in this chapter, most people see their spiritual beliefs as transient rather than fixed. Somehow, children in Christian homes are not grasping the true value of following Jesus—and begin looking for other options soon after they leave home.

- Of those who are married, 37 percent say their spouse has a different religious affiliation.

How are children supposed to get a handle on faith if mom and dad can't agree on one? If one religion is okay for one parent, and another is okay for the other parent, it's natural for our kids to believe there is no right way or wrong way. It's no wonder that moral relativism is so prevalent.

- More than 16 percent of people say they have no religious affiliation whatsoever.

This includes atheists, agnostics, and people who simply don't care. The Bible warns about this, explicitly discussing the danger of becoming "luke-warm." Though Jesus was speaking to Christians, even 2,000 years ago He knew that apathetic people are incredibly difficult to motivate.

- Among 18- to 29-year-olds, 25 percent have no religious affiliation.

At the exact time that America's young people are starting their careers and families, they're abandoning not just their parents' faith, but also faith altogether. Instead of passing along a Christian heritage, today's young families are passing along a faithless heritage.

- People are moving into the "unaffiliated" category three times faster than people are leaving it.

There appears to be a greater incentive (either personally or culturally) to leave your faith, rather than to find one. It doesn't take a rocket scientist to see that within a few generations, the largest religion will be no religion at all.

As if the numbers alone don't tell the story, this is how the Pew Forum describes their results:

> The survey finds that constant movement characterizes the American religious marketplace, as every major religious group

is simultaneously gaining and losing adherents. Those that are growing as a result of religious change are simply gaining new members at a faster rate than they are losing members. Conversely, those that are declining in number because of religious change simply are not attracting enough new members to offset the number of adherents who are leaving those particular faiths.

If that isn't evidence of fair-weather faith, I'm not sure what is. It appears that many people today are content to follow their faith only until it doesn't feel good anymore, the same way football fans are content to root for the New England Patriots until Tom Brady gets hurt, or basketball fans jump on the Cleveland Cavaliers bandwagon until Lebron James leaves town.

What happened to die-hard brand loyalty—regardless of a competitor's sales gimmicks?

What happened to core beliefs—regardless of inconvenience or circumstance?

What happened to truth—regardless of popularity or cultural trends?

The numbers don't lie. People these days are flippantly choosing their faith as if they are buying a pair of shoes or picking a breakfast cereal. We are passionless Christians chasing a passionless culture. And that is a dangerous situation indeed.

4 I Wanted a Honda

How Branding Jesus Works

Perception Is Reality

It may have been Albert Einstein who said that doing the same thing over and over, while expecting a different result is a sign of insanity. In the Christian community, I often wonder if we're experiencing a little bit of that. We're doing what we've always done, without appreciable results. We're following the Sunday school outline from thirty years ago, but aren't seeing any progress. We're beating our collective heads against the wall, wondering why we have a splitting headache.

Over time, two significant changes have occurred in our culture—and neither has been matched with an effective response by Christians. The first is this: Most people no longer think they *need* what Jesus offers. We're a self-reliant world with no desire to follow (or cater to) anybody but ourselves.

The second change is that even if there are some who still see benefits to what Christ offers, most no longer have a favorable perception of who He is (or of those who follow Him). They've been burned by church. They've been hurt by Christians. They've been led to believe that Jesus is a crutch, a fad, or an imaginary friend.

Collectively, these trends mean that Jesus essentially holds no *value* anymore.

In the marketing world, defining *value* can be tricky. The values of some things, like seats at a ballpark or a theater, are based on a single variable—how close they are to the action. While the value of other products, such as T-shirts or jeans, derives from a number of factors.

If you want to watch the Chicago Cubs play at Wrigley Field, the best seats are the most expensive—say $300 for a padded chair behind home plate. Conversely, the worst seats are the least expensive—about $30 for a cozy little slice of bleacher next to the Vienna Beef guy. The cost is directly proportional to the location.

However, when it comes to products like cars and clothes and coffee, the math gets complicated. Expensive cars don't always look better, drive smoother, and last longer than cheaper ones. Identical cotton T-shirts aren't the same price at Banana Republic and at Big Lots. A cup of Colombian doesn't ring up the same at the place that sells frappuccinos and the place that sells fuel.

So when creating ad campaigns for various organizations, I try to simplify things by using this formula:

$$\text{Met Need (MN)} + \text{Favorable Perception (FP)} = \text{Value (V)}$$

If customers feel they need a product *and* they have a positive perception of that product, value is automatically created. That product becomes worth something (money, time, energy). Said another way, for an item to be worth buying, it must not only meet a specific need, but it must also be perceived positively by the potential buyer. And, the greater the need or the perception, the greater the value.

A valued product not only has to do a specific task, but it also has to do it in a way that people like. A janitor who smiles at people and whistles while he works is worth far more than the guy who never makes eye contact and grumbles the whole time. Coach purses, with their extrasoft leather and high-quality latches, are much more valuable than identical-looking generics made with chintzy materials. The advertised innovation behind a Dyson vacuum warrants a higher price tag than the simplicity of the Sears brand. In short, a quality product isn't worth much if potential buyers don't think it is.

Applying faith to this equation then would indicate that for non-Christians to value Jesus, they need to see that He can meet their needs *and* they need a favorable perception of Him. They need both head knowledge and heart feeling. They need information and inspiration. One side without the other is useless. Or in this case, worthless.

Maintenance Men

Most guys I know are "maintenance men." They change their own oil, sharpen their own lawn mower blades, and build their own sheds. They know how to adjust the gap on their spark plugs, attach the green wire when installing a ceiling fan, and light the pilot light on the hot water heater without blowing up the house.

I am not this kind of guy.

I have electrocuted myself while plugging in a dryer. I have melted jumper cables from attaching them the wrong way. I have flipped a riding lawn mower after hitting a swing set. For many years, when it came to home ownership, my rule of thumb was, "When it's time to clean the gutters, it's time to sell the house." (Thankfully, my wife had those gutter-guard thingies installed a few years ago, which has made me very happy and our real estate agent very sad.)

Given my complete lack of mechanical skills, it won't come as a surprise that I'm very selective when choosing a vehicle. My personal need is to have the cars in our garage work—for a long time—with as little effort on my part as possible. I can handle putting gas in them each week, spraying them off with the hose periodically, and taking them to Jiffy Lube every 3,000 miles. Otherwise I'm simply not mentally or physically equipped to deal with even the most basic maintenance issues.

As an aside, my wife has an entirely different set of needs. As the mom of our two little boys, safety is her number-one priority. She wants a car with stability control, antilock brakes, and air bags. She wants crumple zones, a five-star crash test rating, and the ability to always land right-side up on all wheels—kind of like a cat landing on all fours. But understanding your needs is only half the battle in determining which car holds value to you as a customer. One must also have a favorable perception (FP) of the vehicle to feel good about taking out a four- or five-year loan on it.

Perception, by definition, is "the act or faculty of apprehending by means of the senses or of the mind." Perception is more than just black and white. More than numbers on a page. More than information. More than a single variable.

Perception is everything you know combined with everything you feel. It's the opinions your friends have, the articles you read, the commercials on television. It's the box, the bling, the branding, the buzz. Perception is why people pay $5 for a cup of coffee, $150 for a pair of jeans, or $50,000 for a pickup truck when they could get very similar (sometimes identical) products for far less.

As my most recent car quest began, I was faced head-on with my own perceptions. I wanted a Honda. Their vehicles met my reliability need, and I had a very positive perception of their brand. But on the sidewalk of the local auto mall, directly in front of the giant glass doors, sat an absolutely gorgeous car. It was sporty like a BMW and sleek like a Mercedes. A quick peek in the driver's window revealed Lexus-like luxury and a delicately detailed dashboard.

As I leaned into the car, drooling on the heated, two-tone leather seats, I noticed the emblem on the steering wheel. After a double take, I nearly knocked myself out on the window frame. A Hyundai?

I hated Hyundai. Didn't I? A Hyundai is just a tin can on wheels. The auto industry's generic brand. The dollar-store option. Buying a car from Korea would be like buying a lobster from Oklahoma or a sweater from Florida. It didn't make sense.

Before pulling into the dealership, I knew the facts about Hyundai, yet I had never dreamed about buying one. Hyundai offers the best warranty in America (10 years/100,000 miles). Its vehicles are each five-star safety rated. Many of Hyundai's models have won "Top Pick" awards from places like *Consumer Reports* and *Edmunds.* But because I had never encountered a Hyundai in real life, my negative perception remained. Regardless of what I knew, I still didn't feel good enough about Hyundai to consider looking at one . . . much less to buy one.

I went in wanting a Honda. But four hours later, I drove home in a Hyundai. And I love it.

One Positive Experience

What changed? What did Hyundai do differently the day I bought one of their vehicles than the previous nine years? What about their product caused me to change my mind from overt opposition to their brand to falling in love with it?

Nothing. Literally nothing.

All it took was one positive experience for me to reevaluate everything I thought I knew about Hyundai. It took combining my knowledge with the rest of my senses. It took seeing the car up close. Hearing the purr of the engine. Smelling the leather seats. It took an encounter with a product that was so remarkable, so different, I couldn't possibly ignore it.

I wonder if the world sees Jesus (and Christians) much the way I used to see Hyundai. They know some positive things about Him (or us), but they still don't feel good enough about the product to even consider looking at Him. Without both sides of that equation, Jesus holds no value to them.

The question for you and me is: How can we be that shiny, new Hyundai to someone who sometimes thinks *about* Jesus, but doesn't think much *of* Jesus? How can we be parked in the right place at the right time? How can we turn the head of somebody who's not even looking for us? Could a friend's or family member's perceived value of Jesus skyrocket with one simple encounter?

What will it take on our part to encourage a person looking for earthly satisfaction to drive home instead with eternal salvation?

Approval Is Useless

Shortly after the model rolled off the assembly line, Toyota was forced to recall the 2010 Lexus GX 460. Despite passing both government and internal safety tests, the GX was found by *Consumer Reports* to be "unsafe to buy"—apparently because of a high rollover risk.

The National Highway Traffic Safety Administration (NHTSA) does rollover tests on every vehicle that hits showrooms, and their primary test is called the "fishhook." In this test a mechanical arm drives the SUV in a straight line, accelerating to 50 miles an hour. Then it makes a left, followed by a sharp right. If the inside wheels lift two inches or more off the ground, the NHTSA considers the vehicle unsafe. Otherwise, it passes.

This controlled, robot-executed test is a fair test I suppose, but it's a flawed test.

Every car company in the world, including Toyota, is well aware of the fishhook. They know the standards their vehicles have to meet to get the rollover seal of approval. Designers understand that if they can engineer a car or truck to not flip during the fishhook test—as with the Lexus GX 460— they're good to go.

The problem is that, in real life, no two situations are ever the same. With different drivers, pavements, and weather conditions, there are countless ways to flip a car. The fishhook method tests one. It wasn't until *Consumer Reports* put an actual person behind the wheel of the GX 460 in actual driving conditions that anyone realized there was a problem.

How many of us are the same way when it comes to our faith? We've been tested only in a controlled environment. It's easy to say the right things at church, do the right things in our Christian schools, or know the right answers at Bible study. But what happens when we step out into the real world, where situations aren't so cut-and-dried?

Like Toyota, so many of us have learned how to pass. We do just enough to look good. We know how to play the part to get our spiritual seal of approval, yet aren't prepared to be effective in real-life conditions.

As non-Christians begin investigating what Jesus is all about, it's not really *Him* they're testing . . . it's *us*. They're looking at our lives to see if we live up to all the hype. They're looking at our attitudes when life throws us a curve that wasn't on the test. I've never been able to track down who said it first, but one of my favorite quotes is, "People are like tea bags. You find out what's really inside when you put them in hot water." How true. *Good*

As the Lexus GX 460 has shown us, approval is useless if all we do is get out on the road and start hurting people.

5 The Culture Club

Why Branding Jesus Is Difficult

Everything Is Bigger in Texas

With few exceptions, my parents have lived their entire lives in the Midwest—Michigan and Illinois primarily. Growing up, we were a thick-crust-pizza-eating, pop-not-soda-drinking family that dangled our prepositions and talked about corn and soybeans. It wasn't unusual to hear one of us ask, "Hey, can I go with?" or "I wonder if the corn will be knee-high by the Fourth of July this year."

In the little town where our family spent eighteen years, traffic jams were caused by slow-moving farm equipment, and the skyline was made up of an aging silo, a lonely stoplight, and a glowing Hardee's sign out near the interstate. You could get anywhere in about three minutes, and it was nearly impossible to visit the grocery store without seeing someone you knew.

Several years ago, however, my parents moved to Austin, Texas, and suddenly everything changed. Within weeks, Mom and Dad were eating barbeque and corn bread, talking about cotton and tumbleweed, and using the word "ya'll" in everyday conversation. It was like fifty-five years of Midwest living had vanished in a few days.

Though the change wasn't subtle, the extent of their morph wasn't completely evident over the phone. It took their weeklong visit back to Illinois for me to realize how strong the Texas culture really was . . . and how much it had changed them.

While chatting in the driveway with some old friends, my mom looked at a house down their former street and said, "Hey, it's the star of Texas!"

What? Where? Is there such a thing?

Five houses away, dangling from the side of somebody's garage, was a large metal star. It was five-pointed and painted maroon. I've since been told that some people call them "country stars," but you can find one hanging in most every neighborhood in America. Rural or not. To my mom though (now a Texan), it wasn't just a star—it was a *Texas* star.

Apparently, in the Lone Star state, putting a star on their flag and on the 50-yard line of their football stadium means that Texans invented the thing. Maybe I'm naive, but I can't recall ever hearing a Canadian claim ownership of every maple leaf on the planet, or the Japanese try to commandeer the circle. Even the socialists in the USSR didn't attempt to take credit for the hammer. But Texas is different.

After a bit of research, I learned Texans have a history of big thinking:

- Texas was its own country from 1836 to 1845.
- The Capitol Building in Austin was intentionally built seven feet higher than the U.S. Capitol in Washington, DC.
- Legend has it that the Texas flag is the only state flag that can be flown at the same height as the American flag.
- One ranch in Texas (The King Ranch) is larger than the state of Rhode Island.

"Everything's bigger in Texas" isn't just the unofficial state slogan, it's a way of life. *The* way of life. Whether you're born there or you move there, eventually the culture catches up with you.

The lesson to be learned is that our worldview—the lens through which we look at life—affects everything we do. It affects how we spend our time, how we spend our money, what we wear, what we drive, who our friends are, and even what we believe (and why we believe it).

A person's worldview is obviously a complex combination of factors. It's too complex to fully analyze here. However, some of the primary determinants are where one lives (country, state, city, neighborhood), what education one has (public, private, university, trade school), who one's parents are (black, white, young, old), and when one was born (1940s, '60s, '80s, '00s).

The lens through which a gay man in his thirties from San Francisco looks at life will be radically different than a 55-year-old, married woman from Alabama or a public high school student from Chicago's South Side. A Harvard-educated engineer from Massachusetts won't see things the same way as a high school dropout from Los Angeles or a nonprofit attorney from Miami.

The hardest part for Christians to grasp is that, even though we might not "get" a specific culture or worldview, our inability to understand it is completely irrelevant. A person's lens is that person's reality, and it's a reality that we must be prepared to speak to (and through) if we hope to effectively share Christ.

A Change Will Do You Good

Just like Texans and doctors and high school dropouts are known for certain things, Christians are also known for certain things. Randomly choose someone on the street and ask, "How can you tell if people are Christians?" and you'll likely hear at least one of these statements:

- They worship on Sunday mornings.
- They dress up to go to church.
- They put money in the offering plate each week.
- They pray before meals and at bedtime.
- They get up a little early each morning to read the Bible.

Now contrast the above lifestyle with that of average twenty- or thirty-somethings:

- They sleep in on Sunday mornings.
- They wear their best clothes to the club on Saturday night.
- They put as much money in their pocket as possible.
- They pray when there's a cop behind them.
- They rarely (if ever) get up earlier than they have to.

Truth be told, the stereotypical Christian lifestyle is far different from most every other. And I think it's fair to say we take pride in being set apart. We relish the idea of sticking out like sore thumbs. That's a healthy (and biblical) perspective, to a point, but it can become destructive when we start believing it's the "different-ness" that changes our life.

It's really the other way around, isn't it? As people's lives are changed, they then choose to be different. Living a better lifestyle doesn't inspire us to draw closer to God. Drawing closer to God inspires us to live a better lifestyle.

When it comes to sharing Christ with those who (in our minds) are a little "rough around the edges," we're tempted to try to make them look different before they really are different. We're tempted to put them in a tie, shine their shoes, and bring them to church with the hopes that acting the part will help them live the part. But that's no different than putting a cowboy hat on a surfer dude with the hope that he'll develop a southern accent. It's crazy.

Maybe it's all those house-flipping shows on HGTV or makeover programs on ABC, but most people I know love finished projects. We enjoy seeing the before-and-after pictures, but aren't so fond of the process in between. It's too messy. People ask too many questions.

And so we feel the need to cover up that middle part, or at least explain away the work in progress.

I suppose this tendency makes sense. Christians traditionally don't leave much room for transition—despite the fact that we're all in it in one form or another. To be accepted in many Christian circles, if someone is smoking, he'd better be on fire. If someone has a tattoo, there had better be a cross in it. If someone's in rehab, it better be for that knee injury she got playing church softball.

What's the bottom line? Christians often try to change a person's culture rather than let God change her heart. We try to force others to act like us, with the hope that they'll eventually believe like us. That's entirely backward. Heart changes lead to a change in actions, not the other way around.

In many cases I think these Christian tendencies are a form of self-preservation. We would rather bring people onto our turf (where we're comfortable) than step onto someone else's. We would rather alter their lifestyle, culture, and habits, instead of change our routine. Subconsciously maybe we fear we'll be eaten alive if we venture outside what we consider safe territory.

Jesus is bigger than the Christian culture-bubble you and I have put Him in. He can reach people anytime, anywhere. Not just Sunday mornings at 9:30. Not just when people have started doing or saying the "right" things. Not just once people have turned their backs on their culture.

It's not our job to present a perfect person to Jesus—but to present a perfect Jesus to people. When it comes to sharing Christ, attempting to convince a friend to stop getting drunk or sleeping around or cheating on his taxes is counterproductive. Those physical changes will come after a spiritual change has been made. Once God has hold of a person's heart, the head will naturally follow.

I'm Lovin' It

I don't think I'm giving away any proprietary information when I tell you that McDonald's segregates its advertising. They have black commercials and white commercials. Bass-bumping, slang-speaking ads and sweet-sounding, phonetically-flat ads. Radio spots that use words like "vibin'" and "cravin'" and radio spots that don't.

As the voice for some of the company's regional radio and television pieces, I regularly see scripts with the code AACM in the upper right corner. From what I understand, the acronym is strictly used for internal identification purposes but, yes, the AA stands for African-American. The spots are, to say the least, urban, and the voice-overs are supposed to be young, hip, and, well . . . black. There's no other way to put it.

While this may sound like a racist strategy by one of the world's largest fast-food chains, it's really not. McDonald's knows it's foolish to think African-Americans will show up at their restaurants if the company doesn't appeal to their distinct cultures in some of its advertising. The same is true in reverse. Mickey D's wouldn't get many white customers if none of its ads, promotions, or meals appealed to Caucasians and their various cultures.

Culture isn't limited just to race though. As we've discussed, there are thousands of subcultures: young and old, educated and free-spirited, athletic and artistic, agnostic and Christian, gay and straight, Southwest and Northeast. The list could go on forever.

All men and women are created equal, but they are not created the same. Each of us responds differently to images, words, colors, and music. No matter your cultural background, you're far more likely to respond to a message if it's presented in a way you can relate to.

It's why husbands bring flowers to their wives to say "I love you," rather than motor oil. And why women take men out to dinner after the big promotion, not to the ballet. It's why Abercrombie uses sex to sell clothes, rather than puppies. And why Purina uses puppies to sell dog food, rather than sex. McDonald's understands this concept and uses a variety of methods to bring a variety of cultures to the same place—their restaurants.

As Christians, we can't expect to bring a variety of people to Jesus without using a variety of methods either. (Again, we're talking about *tactics*, not mission.) College students aren't going to respond the same way baby boomers do. Singles won't resonate with the same ideas as married couples. Engineers aren't going to gravitate to the same topics as authors.

In 1 Corinthians 9:20–22 (NIV), Paul says:

> To the Jews I became like a Jew, to win the Jews. To those under the law I became like one under the law (though I myself am not under the law), so as to win those under the law. To those not having the law I became like one not having the law (though I am not free from God's law but am under Christ's law), so as to win those not having the law. To the weak I became weak, to win the weak. I have become all things to all people so that by all possible means I might save some.

Here's my personal interpretation of how these verses might have been written today:

> To the Texans I became like a Texan, to win the Texans. To those who are agnostics, as an agnostic, though I myself am not an agnostic, so as to win those who are agnostic. To those who are at the bars I became like one who is at the bars, so as to win those who hang out at the bars. To the homeless I became homeless, that I might win the homeless. I have become all things to all people so that by all possible means I might save some.

Paul knew that he wasn't going to reach everybody with his message, but he did know this—to be effective at sharing the gospel with some, it was critical that he knew who his audience was. It was imperative that he relate to a person's culture. The same is true for you and me.

6 The Product Isn't the Problem

Where Branding Jesus Has Gone Wrong

Hungry, Hungry Hypocrites

In business, when sales of a product or service aren't living up to projections, there are several potential culprits. First on the list is always the product itself. Is it something people feel they need? Does it fulfill that need in a remarkable way (easily, quickly, cheaply)?

After years of beating shirts on rocks and washboards, women decided they needed a quicker, more efficient way to wash their clothes. When the washing machine was invented, their need was met, and (over time) the appliance has been sold to nearly every family in America. A more recent example is the cell phone. As a culture, we felt the need to communicate while we were on the road. Motorola (and others) provided us a way to do that, and the rest is history.

But if a product successfully meets a specific need (as do the washing machine and cell phone), then the evaluation process moves on to the marketing and sales departments. Do potential customers know the product exists? Do they understand what the product does? Once they see it, is it obvious how the product would dramatically impact their lives?

Working in radio, I struggled for years with opening shrink-wrapped CD cases. I used my fingernails, scissors, knives, even my car keys, to try to get those crazy things open. Once I finally did remove the plastic, the CD case usually looked like it had been attacked by a large, angry ferret.

One day a friend showed me a tiny, circular device (appropriately called a CD opener) that changed my life. It had been around for years, but (somehow) I had never heard of it. This little round piece of brilliance had a tiny blade in the center and fit perfectly along the outside edge of a CD. When I ran it along all four sides, the shrink-wrap literally fell off. The thing couldn't have cost more than 20 cents to produce—and it met my needs perfectly. I bought ten of them.

When it comes to Jesus, I think it's safe to say the product isn't the problem. Jesus offers comfort for the brokenhearted. Rest for the weary. Strength for the weak. Healing for the sick. Peace for the stressed. Hope for the hopeless. I don't know of a person alive who couldn't use these things once in a while.

So the evaluation process must move on to Jesus' marketing team. Us. You and me. It's hard to admit sometimes, but Christians (as a whole) are ruining the world's appetite for Jesus. We are often the ones standing in the way of Christ, despite our best efforts to lead people *to* Him.

During the summer of 2009, in an odd twist of fate, two American entertainment icons breathed their last breath—Michael Jackson (50) and Farrah Fawcett (62). One was a "king." The other an "angel." One was played on millions of radios around the world. The other was taped to millions of bedroom walls. One was known for a glove. The other was known for a hairstyle.

For several mornings after their untimely deaths, we discussed the two situations on my radio show. Once in a very factual fashion and once as a lead-in to ask, "Who do you need to love on today before it's too late?"

While the response was fairly positive, here is a sampling of the comments I received via phone, e-mail, and Facebook from our predominantly Christian audience:

- "Why are you promoting a pedophile?"
- "Our family almost turned off the radio. Talking about Michael Jackson is not family friendly."
- "I think it's sad that Farrah Fawcett isn't getting the recognition she deserves because a troubled man like Michael Jackson died."
- "Michael Jackson reminds me of my secular days. Why do we have to bring him up?"
- "So a child molester died. Who cares?"

Complaints for mentioning Michael Jackson—at least a dozen.

Complaints for mentioning Farrah Fawcett—zero.

Sure, Michael Jackson was eccentric. He had seemingly unhealthy relationships with children (though he was acquitted of molestation). He was likely addicted to plastic surgery and painkillers. He was a recluse and very insecure. He was bankrupt. He once dangled his young son over a balcony to show him off to the paparazzi below.

Apparently those things are worthy of stone-throwing.

Correct me if I'm wrong, but Farrah Fawcett wasn't exactly the epitome of morality either. She got divorced. She then lived with a man who wasn't her husband for years. She had a baby out of wedlock. She's most famous for a picture of her in a semirevealing red bathing suit. She posed for *Playboy*—twice.

Rocks? What rocks?

I'm annoyed by the arbitrary lines that Christians draw. I'm annoyed that some of us make ourselves feel better by ostracizing others. I'm annoyed that we pay far more attention to the speck-sized problems of others, rather than the plank-sized problems in our own lives. I'm annoyed that the world pays close attention as we randomly choose who is worthy and who isn't. I'm annoyed that much of the world has no problem with Christ, but has a big problem with Christians.)

But I'm not surprised. And that annoys me too.

In the Bible, when a woman caught in adultery was brought before Jesus, many of the religious leaders wanted to stone her. But Jesus said, "Let any one of you who is without sin be the first to throw a stone at her" (John 8:7 NIV).

The only perfect man to ever walk the planet didn't even condemn this woman. Instead he told her, "Go now and leave your life of sin." What an example! Why is it that many Christians are so quick to accept grace, but are so slow to hand it out?

I'm not asking anyone to embrace Michael Jackson's lifestyle or music, but I am suggesting that the mere mention of his name and accomplishments is not inherently evil. No, Michael wasn't perfect. Neither was Farrah. And neither am I—and neither are you.

If it's not "Christian" to talk on the radio (or write) about people who have fallen short of God's perfect plan, then I should probably find a new line of work. And I should probably duck.

The Fine Print

We currently have two toddlers in the house, so my wife and I buy a *lot* of Cheerios. They're relatively healthy. They don't make too big of a mess. They can be eaten with bare hands straight out of the box. Plus, we can give them to the kids.

Anyway, in big, bold print on the front of the Cheerios box, General Mills now claims their cereal can "help lower your cholesterol." Sounds great, doesn't it? Pull out your magnifying glass, though, and you'll see there's more to the story. To get the best results, the fine print says that Cheerios need to be "eaten as part of a diet low in saturated fat and cholesterol."

Basically, Cheerios will help lower your cholesterol if you eat other foods that are proven to help lower your cholesterol. Brilliant. (As an aside, listening to smooth jazz and engaging in underwater basket weaving can also lower your cholesterol if you're eating a diet low in saturated fat and cholesterol.)

General Mills' bold claims, and subsequent fine print, aren't unusual. Weight-loss companies, work-from-home employers, and debt-reduction businesses frequently use the same tactic. They promise the moon, and then explain the details in really tiny letters or quickly spoken words.

Do their products work? For the most part, yes. But *you* have to do some work too. Sometimes a lot of it.

Eating Cheerios can be a great way to start lowering your cholesterol, as long as you're also willing to step away from the fries and toward fresh fruits and veggies. You really can make six figures working part-time from home, but it's going to mean turning off Oprah and turning on your entrepreneurial skills.

It's not what we want to hear, but it's the truth.

As Christians, it feels like we often give people the idea that Jesus is a magic bullet to a carefree life. We hope that the big, bold smile on our faces will convince our friends and co-workers to try Him—without ever pulling out the magnifying glass and showing them the messiness that following Christ often involves.

In the book of Jeremiah (29:11), the Bible says that God wants to give His people "a future and a hope." But it says nothing about a free ride. Nothing about an easy go of it. Anyone who has been a Christian for longer than an hour knows that—but for some reason, we continue to market Jesus otherwise.

Again, it's not what we want to hear, but it's the truth.

Does Jesus work? Sure, He does. But to get the best results, *we* have to do some work too. Telling people anything else is doing them, and Christianity, a disservice.

Genie in a Bottle

In business, the age-old rule is, "under-promise, over-deliver."

Say that the product is going to take seven to ten business days to arrive, but get it there in four. *Tell* your advertiser that the spot will run for three weeks, but bonus them an extra week. Explain that the tires won't be done until five, but have the car washed and waiting with a carnation on the dashboard when the customer arrives.

Exceed expectations and you win every time.

I follow Donald Miller on Twitter, as do tens of thousands of other people. He's the author of *Blue Like Jazz* and *A Million Miles in a Thousand Years*. In a 2010 tweet, Don beamed about an experience he just had:

> @donmilleris My Kindle stopped working, and Amazon shipped a new one, asking me to return the old in the provided box. Pretty great customer service.

Amazon exceeded Mr. Miller's expectations. They provided him with a better fix for his digital book reader than he was hoping for. In return, Donald Miller provided Amazon with a celebrity endorsement of their service—completely unsolicited and completely free.

One of my favorite companies, not to mention restaurants, is Chipotle. Not only is the food fresh, fast, and absolutely fabulous, but the service is amazing as well. The first time I visited one of these restaurants was because of the recommendation of a friend from work. I was immediately impressed after I walked through the doors. Not only did the young woman behind the counter stuff my fajita burrito incredibly full of meat, cheese, and veggies, but she stuffed it so full that the tortilla broke open—twice. Each time, without hesitation, she got another tortilla and rewrapped my order. Simple, yet remarkable.

Experience tells me that most fast-food employees would ignore the tear in the tortilla, shove the food in a to-go bag, and let me realize the problem once I was in my car with a lapful of hot sauce. But not at Chipotle. Chipotle over-delivered—big-time. In exchange, I'm telling you about it.

Chipotle's customer service approach even extends to its website and iPhone application. Online ordering is quick and easy with both, and using them allows you to skip to the front of the line once you get to the store. However, one afternoon when I went to pick up my three steak tacos, they weren't quite ready. I waited for no more than sixty seconds before an employee approached me, bag in hand. She said, "Sorry. I didn't see your order right away. It came through on the fax machine." *The fax machine? How could that happen?* I wondered. *I don't even own a fax machine.*

After a little investigation, I found out that the local Chipotle franchise was having problems with its computer system that day. When I placed my order at Chipotle.com, a connection couldn't be made between the corporate servers and the local computers. But instead of telling me about the technical glitch (or refusing the request altogether), my order was automatically faxed to the store. Chipotle over-delivered—and didn't even plan to tell me about it!

Again, it was simple, yet remarkable.

It feels like Christians sometimes get this business principle backward. We "over-promise, under-deliver." Hoping to attract new converts, we put God and Christianity in a bright, shiny box full of over-hyped claims and unrealistic ideas—only to leave people disappointed when God doesn't make them healthy, wealthy, and wise.

I can hear you asking, "Is it really possible to over-promise what God can do?" No. It isn't. But it is possible to over-promise what God *will* do.

There's a huge difference.

Many Christians give the impression that God is like a genie in a bottle. The big guy in the sky who holds our "get out of hell free" card.

God is a *healing* God. But that doesn't mean He's going to heal you.

God is a *giving* God. But that doesn't mean He's going to pad your bank account.

God is a *loving* God. But that doesn't mean He's going to take away all your problems.

Over-promising in business leaves customers disappointed. Even angry. They expected one thing, but received a lesser thing.

Over-promising is different—and far more dangerous—when it comes to our faith. Giving people the impression that God will heal you, make you rich, or make your life easier when you become a Christian isn't just over-promising, it's lying. And it's a lie with eternal implications.

I recently heard the story of Emily and Steven. This young couple was anxiously awaiting the birth of their second child when, four months before Emily's due date, the doctor told them Baby Faith wouldn't survive. When asked to consider aborting the pregnancy, Emily and Steven flatly declined. They weren't about to take a life-and-death decision out of God's hands and put it in their own.

After months of carrying a baby she had been told she would never bring home, Emily went into labor and Baby Faith was born—alive. But she didn't stay that way for long. Faith spent nearly two days hooked up to hoses and monitors and needles until nothing more could be done. After a few short hours cradled in her mother's arms, Faith died.

I know that's not how you wanted the story to end. It's not the way I wanted it to end either. If we were in charge, Faith would be alive. If we had written the script, Emily and Steven would be able to tell a remarkable tale of God's faithfulness. They would have been granted a miracle in exchange for doing the right thing, and as a result countless people would have come to Christ.

But that's not how it happened. God had something different in mind. A better plan. A painful plan to be sure, but a better one. Even if Emily and Steven never learn what that plan was.

God doesn't promise health and wealth. Christians do.

We're lying. And our lies aren't attracting people to Christ; they're pushing people away.

Five Types of People to Avoid

Jesus' image problem isn't solely a result of *what* Christians are saying, but also of *how* we're saying it. I don't know about you, but there are five types of people I try to avoid at all costs:

1. Telemarketers. They're pushy, impersonal, and always seem to call at inconvenient times. In fact, so many people dislike telemarketers that Congress passed a law against them.
2. Typical car salesmen. These guys are slick, polished, and use every trick in the book to get you to rush your decision. They'll often tell you whatever you want to hear to make the sale.
3. *People who get in touch only when they need something.* You know the kind. These are people who call or e-mail when they want you to loan them money or join a pyramid marketing company, but vanish otherwise.

4. *Lurkers.* They loiter around ongoing conversations, waiting to inter-ject something irrelevant that steers the discussion toward whatever *they* want to talk about—usually themselves.
5. *God's gift to the planet people.* Those who think they're "it" in terms of their knowledge, looks, or experience. They're better than you, and they aren't afraid to let you know it.

The similarity between each of these types of people can be described in three words: *lack of relationship.* They have an agenda. They want some-thing from you, without offering anything in return. They're trying to fill a personal need at your expense.

Christians often fall into one or more of these categories. Somehow, under the guise of leading people to Christ, we blow off the importance of relationships and begin interjecting our Jesus-agenda whenever possible. We show up unannounced. We have memorized responses to every rejec-tion. We turn every subject into a God-thing. (*"Did you see that hockey game last night? Yeah, that goalie had some amazing saves. Speaking of saved . . ."*) We try to make it seem like *we* have the answers, and *they* don't.

Just because you're sharing your faith doesn't mean you can throw social etiquette out the window. It should be exactly the opposite.

Rotten Fruit

Mere days after Focus on the Family announced they would be airing a pro-life ad during the 2010 Super Bowl, the National Organization for Women came out against the spot . . . immediately demanding that CBS refuse to run it. When I heard NOW's reaction, some less-than-friendly adjectives for these women jumped to mind: hateful, whiny, intolerant, bitter, and pushy—to name just a few.

It seems the only time I hear about this women's rights group is when they're mad about something. Protesting something. Boycotting something.

Calling for legislative action to force anyone who doesn't agree with them to conform to their standards.

Kind of like Christians do.

I'll let that sink in a minute.

It's sad but true. Christians, like many social or political action groups, are often known more for what they're against, rather than what (and Who) they're for.

If the world views us the way I view many of them (hateful, whiny, intolerant, etc.), it won't matter what we say. Our words will never be heard. We'll be written off before we can open our mouths—labeled as crazies or extremists or whatever.

The Bible calls love, joy, peace, and patience the "Fruit of the Spirit," not hate, whinyness, intolerance, and bitterness.

Winning by Default

A series of political ads ran recently in Illinois. I have no idea who the candidate was, or what he was running for. All I know is that, based on his advertising, the guy's chances of winning were pretty much zero.

In a strong, almost agitated voice, this politician took thirty seconds to outline the negative aspects of every candidate he was running against: This opponent supported Barack Obama, that guy got caught using campaign funds illegally, that other guy might be gay—you've seen it all before.

The worst part wasn't the negativity. It was the complete lack of positivity and direction. The spots said nothing about the candidate himself. No qualifications, no policy, no background, no plans for the future—nothing.

This guy's idea, apparently, was to win by default. Cut everybody else down, with the hopes of being the last man standing. It doesn't work that way. Not in politics. Not in business. Not in faith.

To effectively influence people, you have to stand for something. You have to represent something. You have to *be* something.

People don't vote or buy or accept things based on what they aren't. They vote and buy and accept things based on what they *are*. Including Jesus. Especially Jesus.

7 Spiritual Cereality

Why Branding Jesus Is Necessary

The Cereal Aisle

Burger King's old slogan sums up today's culture pretty well: "Have it your way." We're accustomed to having options, with nearly every industry bending over backward to accommodate our ever-changing wishes. Television, which once included just NBC, CBS, and ABC, now has hundreds, probably thousands, of channels, depending upon whether you have satellite or cable. Ford, GM, and Chrysler are now competing with Honda, Toyota, Nissan, and two dozen other automakers. For years, Sears and JCPenney were the only department stores around. Now? Not so much.

One of the most obvious examples of this, for me, is the breakfast cereal industry. I just went to the Cheerios website—and would you believe there are now twelve varieties of Cheerios? That's right, twelve.

Regular
Honey Nut
MultiGrain
Banana Nut
Cheerios Crunch
Berry Burst

Frosted
Apple Cinnamon
Fruity
Yogurt Burst
Chocolate
Cinnamon Burst

As a kid, I remember two . . . maybe three. Tops.

And Cheerios isn't the only breakfast cereal that is diversifying their brand. The uber-healthy Kashi has twenty-four different cereals. Chex has eight options. Same with Special K. Rice Krispies has five. Raisin Bran? Three.

I could go on.

A generation ago, shoppers had only a handful of options. There was one kind of Cheerios. One kind of Wheaties. One kind of Shredded Wheat. If you didn't like them, you didn't eat breakfast.

At least not at my house.

But these days, hundreds of brightly colored boxes line the shelves, each promising in a 72-point font to improve your heart, lower your cholesterol, give you energy, calm your digestive system, or trim your waistline.

Oh, and taste good too.

Is it just me, or does the average cereal section look like someone poured the Disney Channel and the FDA into a blender and started it without the lid on? Making an informed decision with all those cartoon characters shouting at you is like trying to perform calculus during a drum line rehearsal.

I can't help but wonder if the overwhelming feeling I experience while standing in aisle five is the same feeling many people get when looking for a church to attend or a faith to follow.

There are similarities for sure.

I just Googled "protestant." As it turns out, this book isn't nearly long enough to list all of the varieties. Here are just a few:

Adventist
Baptist
Charismatic
Lutheran
Methodist
Nazarene
Pentecostal
Presbyterian
Reformed

The Catholic church has several different factions. So does Islam. And Judaism. Don't forget about Hinduism, Buddhism, Mormonism, and Scientology.

I could go on.

A generation ago, "faith shoppers" in America had about the same number of options as cereal shoppers. These days, there are hundreds of religions, each promising all sorts of amazing stuff.

A carefree existence
An afterlife
Someone or something to pray to
A belief in a cause bigger than yourself

So, let me ask you this: in a crowded, competitive marketplace, what would make your neighbors, friends, or co-workers choose *your* faith?

Choose *your* God?

We live in a culture in which millions of people believe that Christianity is just another option in the religion aisle. Whether you like nuts, flakes, or chocolate chunks, today you can find the belief system that's perfect for you. Sure, they all taste a bit different. But in the end, they fill you up just the same. Don't they?

Some even have a toy at the bottom of the box.

Why force down Mueslix when you can have Count Chocula? Why crunch your way through Grape Nuts when you can have Frosted Flakes? Why choose Christianity when those other faiths look like so much fun?

For some reason, over time, Christ-followers have put themselves in a boring box. Our packaging (lifestyle) gives the impression that Christianity is more about rules than freedom. More about scowling than smiling. More about losing than living. It's not true, of course . . . or it shouldn't be . . . but that's not what many people think. To them, we're sugarless nuts and flakes in a world of Fruity Pebbles.

Now please don't hear what I'm *not* saying.

I'm *not* saying we should reinvent Christianity or turn it into something it isn't.

I'm *not* saying that we need to water down our message to appeal to a broader audience.

I'm *not* even saying we need to use flashy lights or videos at church . . . or bring Starbucks to every Bible study.

I *am* saying we can't be content to simply set our box of Christian Cheerios on the shelf anymore and expect a sizable number of seekers to randomly pick us out of the crowd.

With Madonna eating Kabbalah Krunch and Tom Cruise on the box of

Scientology Smacks, we can't let the Christian faith and belief system be pushed to the back of the bottom shelf anymore.

Variety Packs

In junior high and high school, cereal was a staple for breakfast. In a small cabinet under our kitchen counter, there were always three choices waiting for my sister and me: Cheerios and Shredded Wheat, along with one box of either Raisin Bran, Corn Chex, Wheaties, or Puffed Rice. Each morning before school, the two of us sat at the table and polished off a bowl or two before heading out the door.

The only exception to our family's cereal routine came during our week-long summer vacations. Mom threw caution to the wind and bought the Kellogg's variety packs. Froot Loops–filled, Honey Smacks–holding variety packs. They were awesome. *us too.*

Not only was each tiny box loaded with sugar, but it was a departure from what we had become accustomed to the other 358 days of the year. Plus, you could rip open the sides and dump your milk right into the package. For a 15-year-old boy and his 10-year-old sister, it didn't get much better than that.

The problem usually came on day five of our trips. This was the point when all the sugary cereals were gone and only Special K, Raisin Bran, and All-Bran remained. After nearly a week of the "cool stuff," neither my sister nor I was very excited about what was left.

Sadly, I've witnessed far too many people approach their faith like I used to approach breakfast. They want fun, not fundamental. They want hype, not health. They want choices, not commitment. Rather than choose the spiritual equivalent of a full-size box of Cheerios or Shredded Wheat, many would rather gather tiny portions of several different faiths and create their own "variety pack." All sugar . . . no substance.

It shouldn't be much of a surprise. Our culture has promoted this kind of feel-good, pick-and-choose lifestyle in every imaginable way for years. Drive-thru restaurants, television, and especially the internet have helped create a society that thinks, "I'm going to get what I want, when I want it—and if I don't, I'll go somewhere else."

In his book *Behind the Glittering Mask* author Mark Rutland makes this point beautifully. He writes a hypothetical dialogue between the archangel Michael and Lucifer as they discuss the seven deadly sins. In their conversation about sloth, Lucifer describes it this way:

> Kings sit sweatless upon cushions of ease while valets and footmen do their bidding. Mercenaries fight wars for kings and jesters entertain them. Just as the king is the god of the jester, noble sons of Sloth are gods of their television sets. They stare dispassionately as the one-dimensional hirelings on the screen fight, kill, consume, die and have sex for their entertainment.

Ouch. He goes on.

> Indeed, the tiny screen shrinks the court jesters to a manageable size and the remote control in the god's hand gives him instant power of life and death over the images.

Today's culture flips through faiths like it's flipping through TV channels. Don't like this? Click. Don't like that? Click. Want more of this? Click. Want less of that? Click. Pretty soon they're back to channel two, starting the process over again.

With every aspect of our lives now "on-demand," society assumes that religion should be the same way. If they're not happy, they'll move on to something that makes them happy. They figure, "Why push through tough stuff or work through uncomfortable situations when I can lie on my spiritual sofa and click my way from one faith to the next?"

Behind the Glittering Mask warns of the slothful person:

> In their activity they will care about nothing. Though they may
> easily discover what is worth killing for, the slothful will know
> that nothing, absolutely nothing, is worth dying for.

If those statements are true, then sharing Jesus with a slothful culture—
with a passionless people—will be very, very difficult.

8 Death of a Salesman

Effectively Advertising Jesus

Spaghetti Marketing

Since the invention of television, corporations have been engaged in sales pitches that are high in volume, but low in return, frequently running millions of dollars' worth of national advertisements spread over months or years. This technique is commonly known as mass marketing, but I call it "Spaghetti Marketing." Essentially, sellers of everything from SUVs to BLTs and panty hose to paper towels throw a bunch of noodles (money) against a wall to see how many stick (how many people become paying customers). Each entity is fully aware that most of the spaghetti will fall to the floor, but they're counting on making a profit—thanks to a few gravity-defying pieces of pasta.

If you're like me, you immediately throw away those window and gutter coupons that come in the baby blue envelopes. You flip past the latenight infomercials for ab twisters. You mute the incessant commercials for that barely legal car insurance. But somebody must be paying attention. Otherwise these companies would all go bankrupt.

Over the past fifty or sixty years, marketers have found that putting a brand in front of as many people as possible is the key to staying in business. The law of averages demands it. If a Ford F-150 ad is seen by ten million people, and just one-one hundredth of one percent buy a new truck because of it, Ford sells a thousand extra trucks. They couldn't care less if 9,999,000 people ignored their commercial.

That's why, in addition to running radio and TV ads, credit card companies hand out T-shirts on college campuses, and insurance providers pass out giant, cardboard fans at football games. Billboards and bumper stickers, funny videos and Facebook groups—they all do the same thing. They put a logo, a slogan, or an idea in front of people's eyes and hope a small percentage of a population's actions will change based on what they've seen.

When it comes to sharing Jesus, Christians have adopted a similar philosophy. Let's call it "Spaghetti Evangelism." We put our beliefs on T-shirts, jewelry, bumper stickers, and social networking profiles and hope for the best. We host pageants and plays and potlucks and cross our fingers that somebody, somewhere latches on. We're well aware that our message mostly falls on deaf ears, but we count on making some sort of heavenly profit based on the few people who respond. We're throwing spiritual spaghetti, and we're praying it supernaturally sticks.

The problem with mass marketing and Spaghetti Evangelism is that they're considered by potential "customers" to be an invasion. These unsolicited messages are lobbed from a seemingly uncaring entity. They're facts and figures without feeling. They're random bits of information without any evidence of transformation. If members of an organization don't care enough to get their hands dirty—if they never show evidence of being personally affected by their own product—why should anyone else care?

While most companies today still use Spaghetti Marketing, many have begun to recognize the shift that is coming (and is already here). This generation's most successful enterprises (Google, Starbucks, Apple, Amazon) have discovered that creating passionate customers and inspiring them to do one-on-one marketing is a far superior way to spread the word about a product, service, or cause.

Passionate customers openly share with their friends. They offer unpaid endorsements to their family members. They use their favorite products proudly and publicly. Instead of a sales pitch coming from some*thing*, these recommendations come from some*one*—and people trump pictures every time. You get more stick, less mess.

It's critical that we understand this concept when sharing our faith. It's vital we recognize just how invasive (and annoying and ineffective) Christians become when we don't first engage in relationship. It's imperative we realize how many noodles could needlessly fall to the floor before we start lobbing linguini at the wall.

Jesus' "brand" is faltering because Christians—those of us who are supposed to be the most passionate about Him—have decided to take the easy way out. We have decided to mass market our Savior, rather than take the time to develop trusting friendships. Christianity is not something that can effectively be sold to the masses. It's not something that can be hawked from afar. Spaghetti Evangelism doesn't work well enough to continue doing it.

Jesus is a *relational* brand, and He requires a *personal* sales approach.

Knowledge Is Not Power

Like most kids his age, my son has a lot of books. They're full of colors and shapes and numbers and animals. And plenty of unidentifiable sticky stuff.

For a while, every time my wife and I read one of these books to our son, we would have to point each item out and tell him what the object was: square, seven, snake. Slowly but surely, Jeremiah would start telling us what was on the page. "Two," he would say. Or "triangle." Or "snot."

As a toddler, Jeremiah didn't really comprehend what the number two or a triangle was. He was simply memorizing pictures he saw in his books. To him, a number was just a squiggly line on paper, not a method for counting. A triangle was just another picture, not a three-sided shape.

All of a sudden one day, things changed.

Jeremiah was playing with his books in the family room. As the little guy opened up a book, he propped it up on the floor so it looked like a tent. Then he did it again with another. Without hesitation, he looked at me and said, "Two triangles."

It was official. Jeremiah had moved from memorization to application.

How many of us Christians are stuck in the memorization stage when it comes to Jesus? We recognize Him when we read the Bible, but find it hard to see Him (or apply Him) in the real world. We know the verse or the parable or the analogy, but we can't quite apply it to the twenty-first century.

For most of my life, I never quite understood what calling God "Father" really meant. Of course I knew what it was supposed to mean. I memorized plenty of verses that described Him as such. But I don't think I could have effectively explained the idea to anyone.

The Lord's Prayer says, "Our Father, which art in heaven, hallowed be Thy name." Tens of millions of people have memorized those words. But how many have any idea what they mean to us, here on earth? For years, I sure didn't.

Then I became a father myself, and I started to get it.

My kids whine a lot. They scream when they want something. They're stubborn and selfish. They specifically do what my wife and I tell them not to do. Yet somehow at the end of the day when I peek in my sons' rooms to turn off the lights . . . I don't care. I love those little guys more than anything. They're a part of me, and regardless of what they do or how they act, I'm going to keep on loving them.

God acting as our Father makes all the sense in the world to me now. It's practical and it's relevant to my everyday life. I mess up all the time. I whine

and scream. I'm stubborn and selfish. Yet at the end of the day, God still)
loves me more than anything.

How can we possibly be effective at sharing Jesus if He's just in our heads
and not in our hands? How can we convey His love, compassion, and for-
giveness to others if we don't really understand how He works?

It's often said that "knowledge is power," but that's not completely true. The
application of knowledge is power.

Polar Opposites

If you purchased a television, camcorder, or piece of audio equipment in
the late '90s or early 2000s, you likely walked into either Best Buy or Circuit
City.

Maybe both.

The differences between the two stores were stark.

Best Buy was the young, hip, fun store where the music blared, the lights
gleamed, and the employees looked the part. The stage was set perfectly,
except for one, glaring problem.

Best Buy employees were clueless.

If you could find one.

Catching up with one of these elusive, blue-shirted creatures usually
required traveling to the deep recesses of the store . . . on your tiptoes . . .
and surprising them in the middle of a courtship ritual with a female member of the blue-shirt kingdom.

After the effects of your blow dart wore off, the conversation usually went
something like this:

You: "I have a question about the televisions."
Employee: "They're over there."
You: "I know, but I need to know which ones have s-video inputs."
Employee: "What's an s-video input?"
You: "Never mind."

Across the street at Circuit City, it was the complete opposite.

Everything about the place felt stodgy. Comparatively speaking, the stores were quiet, dim, and staffed by guys with master's degrees in computer science.

At Circuit City there was never any fear of having to hunt for someone to help you. Within seconds of walking through the automatic doors, a commission-hungry, tie-wearing employee was breathing down your neck asking a series of scripted questions.

Those conversations usually sounded *this* way:

Employee: "Hi! Welcome to Circuit City. Is there anything I can help you find today?"
You: "I have a question about the televisions."
Employee: "Rear projection, LCD, plasma, or tube?"
You: "I just need to know which ones have s-video inputs."
Employee: "Most people mistakenly think that s-video stands for super-video, but it doesn't. There's actually a 4-pin mini-DIN connector as well as a 7-pin locking dub connector. Then, on s-video patch bays, you'll find dual Y and C BNC connectors . . ."
You (fighting off a sudden headache): "Never mind."

Essentially, you were forced to pick your poison. You either wandered aimlessly for twenty minutes looking for mediocre help at Best Buy, or army crawled your way through Circuit City hoping to avoid the enemy combatants.

It's unfortunate, but Christians tend to fall into these same sales categories.

We're either complacent and clueless about those around us who are searching for Jesus, or we're so excited about some sort of heavenly commission check that we can't help but smother anyone who walks by with hyperspiritual churchspeak.

When I was in college at the University of Illinois, Preacher Dan stood on the quad every single day. From the top of his *actual* soap box, Preacher Dan would shout Bible verses, condemn injustices and inequalities in the world, and tell nearly everyone who walked by that they were going to hell unless they repented of their sins.

From what I remember, nothing Preacher Dan said was a lie. Nothing. He was a smart man who knew the Bible well. But like the crew at Circuit City, Dan didn't have a clue how to deliver his message in a relational, relevant way. Instead, he was content to accost unsuspecting college students and quote seemingly random verses to them.

There was a time in our history when electronics stores could afford to operate like this. And there was a time in our history when Christians could too. But that time is over.

If a seeker walks into your church and is ignored, she's never coming back. If a co-worker can't get a word in edgewise without you beating him over the head with the Bible, it's too late. With the myriad of spiritual options out there, people aren't willing to put up with it.

And frankly, they shouldn't have to.

In the business world, Best Buy recognized the problem and decided to make changes. They kept the comfortable atmosphere, but started hiring knowledgeable, passionate salespeople—men and women capable of sharing information in ways that were relevant to Best Buy's customers.

These new employees not only knew the ins and outs of s-video, but (more importantly) could tell you in layman's terms what it was—as well as the quickest way to hook your kid's PlayStation to it.

Circuit City decided to maintain the status quo.

Guess which one is out of business.

The spiritual status quo isn't going to cut it anymore.

Just ask Circuit City.

The Perfect Super Bowl Ad

Google really doesn't *need* to advertise. Like Starbucks and Apple and Amazon, they have passionate customers who spread the word for them. But when Google does advertise, they do it brilliantly. To me, the search engine company's 2010 Super Bowl spot was one of the best I've ever seen. Google's commercial did three things:

1. *It told a story.* A college student goes to study in Paris. Meets a French girl. Falls in love. Finds a job in France. Gets married. Starts a family.
2. *It showed how Google's product works in the real world.* The freshman-turned-family-man used Google to search his way through life's tough questions.
3. *It was simple.* There was no flashy video. No famous actors. No voice-over. Just a computer screen and a few simple sound effects.

It was perfect—and incredibly effective.

As Christians, we advertise Jesus wherever we go. And with a few simple tweaks, we can use these same three steps to share our faith effectively.

1. *Tell your story.* If you're a churchspeak kind of person, this would be your *testimony.* No one can refute what has happened to *you.*

2. *Show how Jesus makes a difference in your everyday life.* Knowledge, facts, and figures are useless unless they benefit your life in some way.

3. *Keep it simple.* Though at times they can be helpful, no flashy lights, videos, tracts, Bible studies, or conferences are required.

The concept is simple, but executing it is not easy. That's why Google pulled it off, and no other company did. Few Christians have mastered the art either.

9 Sweet Emotion

Honestly Sharing Jesus

Cue the Deer

If you've seen the movie *Funny Farm*, you've witnessed—albeit in an exaggerated, made-up sort of way—how difficult it can be to tell a believable story. In the 1988 film, Andy and Elizabeth Farmer (played by Chevy Chase and Madolyn Smith) leave New York City to begin a new chapter of their lives in the country. Andy's dream is to become an author. Elizabeth hopes to start a family. And they plan to do both in the tiny town of Redbud.

Within hours of moving into their old but charming home, the Farmers realize the residents of Redbud are unique at best and crazy at worst. A drunk mailman. An incompetent sheriff. A senile antique store owner. Perhaps *eccentric* would have been a more accurate adjective for these folks.

Mere months later, after a series of incredibly unfortunate events, the once happy couple find themselves on the brink of divorce and ready to sell their used-to-be dream home.

At this point Andy and Liz begin to tell a story. The same story that once sold *them* on the idea of Redbud. The story that said, "Moving into *this* little house in *this* little town will make all your problems go away and all your dreams come true."

For the better part of the movie, the Farmers attempt to turn their house, and their town, into something one might have seen on the cover of the *Saturday Evening Post*. They act, decorate, and dress like figures in a Norman Rockwell painting, and even pay the townspeople fifty dollars each to do the same. They figure, if the right story is in place, the house will sell itself.

One of my favorite lines in the film comes when a young, naive couple is approaching the Farmers' home for the first time. As the potential home-buyers look out over the countryside, Andy peers through a side window—gripping a walkie-talkie. As the two lovebirds head for the front door, Andy forcefully says, "Cue the deer."

Before the prospective homebuyers can ring the doorbell, a once captive fawn gracefully runs from behind the house and across the snow-covered yard, toward the iced-over pond and winding gravel road. You can almost see the words "happily ever after" dancing in the woman's eyes. The caroling townsfolk, the hot cocoa by the fire, and the sobered-up mailman end up merely being icing on the story's cake.

Unfortunately, Andy and Liz Farmer's story was an utter lie. It was a temporary ruse to convince unsuspecting buyers they were purchasing a piece of Americana. A piece of the good life. A piece of their dreams.

In the book titled *All Marketers Are Liars*, Seth Godin outlines nine characteristics of a great story. While each is applicable here, the following are four of my favorites:

1. Great stories are true.
2. Great stories make a promise.
3. Great stories are trusted.
4. Great stories don't contradict themselves.

Notice a theme? Honesty. Godin doesn't use words like "true" and "promise" and "trusted" by accident. A dishonest story isn't really a story at all. It's a trick. A lie. And while it might at first get you your desired result, it's a strategy you will almost certainly regret in the long run.

The story that Christians most often tell is their own. The story of their relationship with Christ. The story of their life since finding Jesus. Their testimony. Unfortunately, I fear many of us aren't telling our stories honestly.

In an effort to sell our faith, we pull a Farmer. We dress up—ourselves, our kids, our homes—to appear like everything is just fine. As if, post-conversion, we're living a dream. As if, miraculously, we've got it all together. When in reality, that's not true at all. We have hope in the middle of trying times. We have a Savior who loves us unconditionally. We have the promise of life after death. But we don't have utopia. Not by a long shot.

When interacting with unsaved friends and co-workers, we Christians often stash our addictions, hide our inadequacies, and gloss over our imperfections so we appear perfect. We figure that if a dream scenario is in place, Christianity will sell itself. But ultimately, our story is a lie. Life isn't perfect. A relationship with Jesus doesn't erase all of our problems.

Rather than opening the door and honestly sharing what a true relationship with Jesus is like—rather than recounting the many times Jesus has had to carry us through the mess we've made of life—we crouch by the window, waiting to "cue the deer."

Storytelling 101

Whether it's a book or a movie, a television show or a musical, every story has one defining characteristic: conflict. It's inevitable. A cheating husband. An enemy combatant. An unrealized love. An underdog. Even children's stories have conflict. Humpty Dumpty couldn't be put back together again. London Bridge fell down. A baby and cradle are blown out of a tree. A little pig went to market. (I'm pretty sure he wasn't going shopping, if you know what I mean.)

Conflict adds excitement and suspense to a story. It keeps the audience wondering what will happen next and guessing how the characters will handle the situation. Without conflict, we wouldn't know who to root for. Without conflict, there would be no distinction between good and evil. Without conflict, I wouldn't cry like a baby every time I watch *Bambi*.

A story without conflict is two things. First, it's boring. If you and I went to see a movie that had absolutely no conflict, we would either walk out or fall asleep. Human beings, by our very nature, identify with conflict. We're able to see ourselves in those stories. What kind of power would *The Ugly Duckling* have if it were *The Pretty Duckling*? How intriguing would *Rocky* be if it were a movie about a CPA? Would anybody remember the *Titanic* if it had missed the iceberg?

The second thing about a story with no conflict is that it's not believable. Nothing is perfect. Nothing *true* anyway. We're fallen beings in a fallen world, and the absence of conflict is an immediate indicator that the words we're hearing and the pictures we're seeing can't possibly be legitimate. Getting wrapped up in a story line requires that we believe what the author is telling us. And if there's no conflict, there's no belief.

So imagine how skeptical non-Christians are when we tell them a perfect story. When we leave our sins, setbacks, and struggles out of the equation. When we wear smiles with our ties or dresses and show the world just how wonderful and problem-free our lives are now that we've found Jesus.

In an effort to make Christ seem more attractive, it's tempting to highlight all the good stuff and none of the bad. To talk with non-Christians about love and joy and fellowship, but not about grace and repentance and fear. To smile and hug and raise our hands without ever crying and doubting and spending time on our knees. It may seem unnatural, but without conflict, our "perfect" lives are telling a tale that can't be believed. And shouldn't be believed.

Whether it feels right or not, there is tremendous power in your conflict. In your divorce. In your drug habit. In your bankruptcy. In your depression. In your grief. As counterintuitive as it may seem, don't hide them. When appropriate, share these struggles openly and honestly. None of your friends want to watch *The Perfect Christian*. It's boring—and it's not believable.

Our friends and neighbors are skeptical enough of Jesus as it is. There's no reason to add to their skepticism by telling a story that couldn't possibly be true.

Compel . . . Don't Coerce

In most cases as we share our lives, I don't think Christians are intentionally trying to be deceptive. Quite the opposite. We're trying to be effective. We're trying to present Jesus in the best possible light to those who might be seeking Him.

The problem is that we're forcing the issue. We're attempting to *make* people believe, rather than make them *want* to believe. There's a big difference.

When you *make* people do something, they act out of fear. An employee works overtime because he's afraid of getting fired. A child cleans her room because she's afraid of being grounded. A wife puts dinner on the table at 5:30 every night because she's afraid of her husband's anger.

With force, you get panic, not passion. You get compliance, not creativity.

But when you make people *want* to do something, they act out of desire. An employee works overtime because he knows his boss gives bonuses to those who show extra effort. A child cleans her room because she knows she'll have extra time to play games before bed. A wife puts dinner on the table at 5:30 every night because she knows her husband plans to take the kids off her hands afterward so she can read a book or take a bath.

Workplaces are more successful, families are more solid, and marriages are more secure when "want to" beats out "have to." When desire beats out fear. That also goes for one's relationship with Christ.

When God created humans, He could have made us robots. He could have forced His creation to follow the master plan. He could have demanded that Adam and Eve obey His every command. But He didn't. God knew that forced love isn't love at all—it's punishment. He understood that mandated allegiance isn't allegiance—it's slavery.

The stories of our walk with Christ are powerful tools, but (no matter how tempting it may seem) we should never use them to try to *make* people accept Jesus. Our job is to tell our stories openly and honestly. To be living examples of the difference Christ can make in a life. To make those around us *want* to believe.

That's how God designed it from the beginning.

10 White Headphones

Passionately Following Jesus

Taking a Bite of the Apple

Not long ago, business experts were writing eulogies for Apple. The computer company was hanging by a thread and seemed ready to fall from the tree. By now, we all know that Apple not only hung on to the tree, but pretty much bought the entire orchard.

In 2003 though, the reality of the situation was that less than 2 percent of people used Apple's computers. Though the Mac brand was held in high esteem by photo and video types, personal computers from Hewlett-Packard, Dell, and IBM had the home (and small business) market cornered.

Mac users, despite being few and far between, loved their machines. They were surprisingly intuitive, extremely stable, and highly efficient. They looked pretty cool too. Unfortunately, 98 percent of the world had no idea. Or, if they did, they didn't feel any of those benefits was a compelling enough reason to switch from a PC.

And those who had an Apple allegiance liked the fact they were different from everyone else. Many even took the attitude that sharing their little secret would ruin the product's exclusivity. Rather than tell other people about the amazing platform they had found, early Mac users were like gold prospectors who had just struck the mother lode. They kept quiet, hoping no one else would stumble upon their discovery.

With that kind of shaky history, how did Apple turn things around and so quickly become one of the world's most recognizable brands? Why was Steve Jobs, Apple's founder, touted by *Fortune* magazine a few years ago as the CEO of the Decade? What turned a nearly bankrupt business into an enterprise with annual sales of more than sixty-five billion dollars?

The first part of the answer is that Apple developed easy-to-use products that made people's everyday lives better. Without a quality product, Apple would never have succeeded. But lots of companies manufacture good stuff. There are thousands of quality companies producing millions of quality products that you and I have never heard of. Quality simply isn't good enough anymore.

The second part of the answer is what too many companies don't do (or can't do). Apple has managed to turn their customers into followers. Turn their followers into fans. And turn their fans into marketers. Customers buy. Followers buy, and then come back. Fans buy, come back, and buy again. Marketers buy, come back, buy again, and encourage everyone around them to buy too.

In his book *Purple Cow,* author and business blogger Seth Godin calls these types of people "sneezers." Like a four-year-old with a cold, when sneezers get hold of a new idea or product, they share it with everyone. And the more they share, the more the concept spreads. (Godin calls anything worthy of sneezing an "ideavirus.")

Apple fans are sneezers.

They'll tell anyone within earshot about the newest app on their iPhone (*ah-choo*) or the song they just downloaded to their iPod (*ah-choo*). They'll show you a video of their kids in the palm of their hand (*ah-choo*) or the GPS map of their family vacation (*ah-choo*).

With all the marketing mucus flying around, you almost can't avoid catching the bug.

But the true brilliance of Apple's back-from-the-grave story is that, even if you've never personally been sneezed on by someone with the Apple flu, you actually have been.

Subliminally.

It takes just a quick glance around a coffee shop or a bookstore to see that iPod and iPhone connoisseurs are set apart from the users of every other MP3 player and cell phone. It's not their spiky hair, their strong cologne, or their well-worn Birkenstocks. It's their white headphones.

That's right. The key to Apple's success lies in the color of their headphones.

It's an amazingly simple and remarkably effective branding technique. Every time you see those bright white cords coming out of someone's ears, you instantly know where that person's technological allegiance lies. Someone is sneezing about Apple without even realizing it.

Sneezing at the airport.

Sneezing in class.

Sneezing on the job site.

Sneezing at the football game.

Millions of times every day, Apple fans unintentionally share their story with potential customers. The story that's being told is more powerful than any TV commercial, billboard, or web review . . . and not just because it's free. Each tale is real. It's honest. It's relevant. As potential customers identify with the story, they become paying customers. Then the process starts all over again. All because of white headphones.

According to the Bible, Christians are supposed to have a spiritual set of white headphones. A unique quality that makes it immediately obvious to the world that we're followers and fans of Jesus.

> And now these three remain: faith, hope and love. But the greatest of these is love. (1 Cor. 13:13 NIV)

> By this everyone will know that you are my disciples, if you love one another. (John 13:35 NIV)

It sounds so simple, and yet today, love is uncommon. It's different. It's remarkable.

St. Francis of Assisi supposedly said it this way, "Preach the gospel at all times—if necessary use words."

When love is authentically lived out, it can be seen both up close and from a distance.

Love is holding open a door and letting go of a wrong. Love is crying with a friend and smiling at a stranger. Love is walking an old lady across the street and sitting with a young boy as he does his homework. Love is mowing your neighbor's lawn on a hot summer's day and shoveling her driveway in subzero temperatures. Love is showing up early to help set up and staying late to help tear down. Love is being slow to anger and quick to forgive.

When people look at you, do they see love? Is it obvious in the airport, in class, at your job, at the football game? Do your friends, family members, and neighbors see you as an apathetic consumer of Jesus who is content to simply *use* Him, or as a passionate follower of Jesus who can't help but *share* Him?

In a world full of selfishness and slander, hypocrisy and hate, love sticks out like a pair of white headphones.

A Big Secret

As humans, our senses are tied together. So the white headphones philosophy is about more than what people see. It's also about what people feel.

BMW gave away that secret recently. On TV. During the Olympics. To 20 million people. Repeatedly. (I suppose it's not a secret anymore.)

The car company's television commercial said plainly, "At BMW we've learned that what you make people feel is just as important as what you make."

I could almost quit right now. That's *huge*. In fact, it's one of the biggest secrets to effectively branding a product or service.

But for most marketers (of cars or anything else), knowing the secret isn't enough. Knowing that it's critical to make your customers *feel* something doesn't help if you can't actually *do* it. As we talked about with Google, doing it is the hard part.

Coke commercials, with their fun music and bright colors, make people happy. The scarred dogs and starving cats in the ASPCA commercials make people sad. VW used sudden crashes in their ads a few years ago to make people scared. The partisan rhetoric in many political spots tries to make people mad. Abercrombie ads use sculpted bodies and sultry music to make people feel, well . . . you know.

The poet Maya Angelou once said, "I've learned that people will forget what you said, people will forget what you did, but people will never forget how you made them feel."

Apple's products are not only amazingly well designed, but they also make people feel. Important. Included. Cool. Connected. Rich. Relevant. Techy. Trendy.

I suppose that's why Jesus works so well. He makes people feel too. Safe. Secure. Whole. Hopeful. Loved. Led. Aware. Accepted. If He were just words on a page, I'm not sure how many of us would want a relationship with Him. And I'm pretty sure He knew that from the beginning.

That's the beauty of a relationship with Christ. It's designed to be a combination of head and heart. Of knowing and feeling. Of what the Bible *says* is true and what we *experience* to be true in our daily lives.

11 Not Every Artist Wears a Funny Hat

Relevantly Showing Jesus

Experience vs. Information

The gleaming car chirps as the salesman unlocks the driver's door and tosses you the keys. You lift the handle and slip into the leather captain's chair. With a slight adjustment of the armrest and the lumbar support, it's almost as if you're sitting in your recliner at home.

A perfect fit.

Maybe it's the new car smell, but the inside seems even more beautiful than the outside. The natural light from the sunroof exposes every spacious corner. Despite the roominess, everything you need is at your fingertips—the stereo, the temperature knobs, the cruise control, and the navigation system.

There's even a special place for your sunglasses. As if you're ever going to take them off.

A slow turning of the key triggers the car to life. Calming blue lights glow on the dashboard, and (though you have to strain a bit) you can hear the purr of the engine. You're even petting the wheel as if it were a real cat.

Smiling, the salesman nods knowingly.

It's obvious you want to take her for a spin.

Out on the road, love is in the air. You gently hold the wheel. You're able to hug every corner as the tires kiss the pavement. In your head, and in your heart, long-term plans are already being made.

You're sold. The dotted line hasn't been signed yet, but you might as well start programming the radio. The honeymoon has started early.

Now, if you'll indulge me a second, let's rewind and go back to the moment you set foot on the car lot.

What would have happened if, after describing your dream vehicle to the salesman, he had walked you to his office instead of the shiny rows of cars? What if he sat you down and began reading you an owner's manual?

"I think I have the perfect vehicle for you," he says.

"Power locks, seats, and windows. Leather interior. Sunroof. The Bose stereo and navigation system come with this model." His droning continues. "It has a 3.5-liter engine with 270 horsepower and more than 100 cubic feet of interior room . . ."

You've been presented with the exact same details as before, but are you sold? Of course not. Are you even interested? Hardly. Knowledge and experience are *not* the same thing.

Jesus is not a car, but He *is* something to be seen, felt, and experienced. And most non-Christians, like car buyers, need to see, feel, and experience Him before understanding the value of the owner's manual. The Bible is necessary, important, and full of incredibly helpful insights and guidelines. But unless a person has actually *seen* Jesus in you and me, God's words aren't going to mean a lot.

(Sometimes I don't think we quite understand this. Our entire lives we've
been taught *what* to say or do, but not *how* to say it or do it.)

In his book *Finding Common Ground*, Tim Downs discusses the problem many Christians have with effectively sharing their faith. Here's how
Downs describes the learning curve of many new believers:

> He learns to do book studies, character studies, and word stud-
> ies. He reaches a substantial level of Christian maturity, but
> he still hungers to grow more . . . In seminary, he delves even
> further into the science of the Bible. He studies systematic the-
> ology, hermeneutical principles, and the original languages of
> the Scriptures . . . [Then] he is granted a title—Master of the
> Knowledge of God. Unfortunately, the Master forgot something
> . . . He has no art.

How could we possibly leave out such an important part of the equation?

Jesus was an artist. He frequently related to people through stories and
analogies. His teachings focused on fields and vineyards and camels passing through the "eye of a needle." Each was extremely relevant to the people
of Jesus' day.

David was an artist too. When writing psalms—songs of praise—he com-
municated through poetry and rhythm and rhyme. Full of passion and
emotion, psalms were a common form of entertainment back then.

Don't get me wrong, information is important, but without some amount of
relevant art, most of today's culture won't care. Not even a little bit. Downs
puts it this way:

> The Christian has accomplished something truly remarkable
> . . . He has taken the most fascinating, life-transforming com-
> munication in the world and made it boring.

Instead of being so anxious to share with nonbelievers our knowledge of Jesus and the Bible, it's important that we are first anxious to show how that information can touch their everyday lives. And share it in a compelling way.

Maybe you're a musician or an author. Maybe you're a good listener or a storyteller. Maybe you're an outdoorsman or a scrapbooker. Maybe you're a financial wizard or an amazing chef. Maybe you're a fearless leader or a merciful lover of people.

It doesn't matter.

Whether you like it or not, you're an artist. And it's time to find your canvas.

Noisy Gongs and Clanging Symbols

As we look for new and relevant ways to show Jesus to today's culture—to be artistic if you will—it's natural to think of evangelizing through social networks like Twitter and Facebook. If hundreds of millions of people flock there daily, shouldn't Christians flock there too?

Just a cursory search of these friend-sharing websites finds that Christians are already there. In droves. On Facebook alone, there are no fewer than 80,000 Jesus-oriented fan sites, with titles including "Jesus Saves," "What Would Jesus Do?" and "Let's See If Jesus Can Get More Fans Than Justin Bieber." (He can, by the way.) There are thousands more sites that condemn abortion, homosexuality, and the occult. One poll I saw the other day even asked me to vote on whether I thought atheists and agnostics were going to hell. Wow.

Is this really how millions of Christ followers think they're going to turn people to Him? Is this really how Jesus imagined His name would be spread? Is this really the best culturally relevant way to impact our friends and co-workers?

The effort, I suppose, is admirable. But it seems to me that social networks are just another convenient, embarrassment-free way to stand up for our faith. They're a newer, hipper version of the Christian T-shirt or the "abortion kills" bumper sticker. They're the hands-off, hassle-free way to feel better about not really impacting anyone for Jesus in person. (Remember "Spaghetti Evangelism" from chapter 8?)

This point was solidified for me as I drove home from work the other day, behind the epitome of a "man truck." This dual-exhaust, dual-wheel pickup was loud, large, and covered with odes to the owner's manliness: stickers about fishing and hunting, camouflage in the back window, and the (seemingly obligatory) masculinity symbol hanging from the hitch.

Perhaps unknowingly, the driver was telling me who he was—without ever opening his mouth. He was creating a first impression without ever looking me in the eye. He was pushing me away before I had the chance to get close. From hundreds of feet away, it was clear that his interests, values, and personality couldn't be more different from mine.

In truth, there's every chance this guy was a really cool person. If we had pulled into the same gas station, there's a possibility we could have struck up a conversation. Even become friends. Maybe, over time, he could have inspired me to bait a hook or taught me how to load a gun. Instead, his symbols told me that if we both happened to stop at the Shell station, I should probably use the pump at the other end.

I'm all for self-expression. But it has become painfully obvious to me that these symbols, these random statements of belief, are incredibly counterproductive. While it seems reasonable to think that shiny jewelry or Facebook pages or yard signs will attract people to us (or to our cause), it's really just the opposite. The only people attracted by these attention-grabbers are people who already act, think, or believe like us. They preach to the choir and push everyone else away. They further insulate us from the world by burying us even more deeply among our own kind.

Christians are notorious for their symbols, and social networks are just the latest version. Before Facebook and Twitter we relied on T-shirts with popular logos morphed into Christian sayings. Necklaces and earrings with crosses. Bumper stickers proclaiming, "Jesus is the Way." Bracelets asking what Jesus would do. We've told ourselves that these displays will open doors to talk with our friends and co-workers about Christ. But they almost never do.

Think about the last time you saw the Christian fish symbol (*icthus*) on the back of someone's vehicle. Did you immediately feel bonded to them as a fellow follower of Jesus? If you're a Christian, probably so. Now think about the last time you saw the ichthus-with-legs symbol on a car. My guess is that, due to the driver's obvious evolutionary beliefs, you likely developed some not-so-positive opinions. The Christian fish attracts creationists and repels evolutionists, while the Darwin fish accomplishes the opposite. Our symbols *don't* bring people from one side to the other. Yet we continue to pretend they do.

Symbols say far more about you and me than they say about Jesus. They say we want only those people to approach us who are already interested in what we have to say. They say we prefer to lob our beliefs at others from afar. They say that, rather than develop loving, caring, trusting relationships with people, we plan to let our shirts, jewelry, and social network profiles do the talking for us.

Unlearning the Lingo

Having been a Christian since I was four, my head is full of an inordinate number of pointless words and phrases. Things that no one outside of the Christian community understands. In fact, many people inside the faith don't comprehend them either.

We can be artistic all we want, but if nobody understands the art, it's useless. If we use analogies, stories, or terminology that require a translation from someone who attended vacation Bible school back in the 1980s, we might as well pull out our flannelgraph board and fuzzy-backed cutout Jesus. Being relevant to a world unfamiliar with Christ will require unlearning many of these insider (dare I say archaic) methodologies.

I'm not trying to pick on anyone, but "traveling mercies" is one of my favorite Christianese phrases. Instead of praying for a safe trip to grandma's house, we say, "Please pray for traveling mercies as we visit family this weekend."

Technically speaking, *traveling* means "making your way from one place to another" and *mercy* means "not getting something you deserve." Put the two together and praying for "traveling mercies" is saying that when Christians go on road trips, we *should* get hit by a bus or run off the road, but we're hoping we don't.

Perhaps all of those Sunday school songs from way-back-when jaded us. Remember these?

> Climb, climb up Sunshine Mountain,
> heavenly breezes blow . . .

or . . .

> Deep and wide, deep and wide,
> there's a fountain flowing deep and wide . . .

With lyrics like those, you would think we could find heaven by hoofing our way through western Colorado or that God's love is like Chicago's Shedd Aquarium. What in the world are we thinking? Being called a "fool for Christ" is one thing, but actively making a fool of ourselves is completely unnecessary.

I know it's easy to laugh at some of these examples, but the problem is real. When relating our faith to a culture that's completely unfamiliar with it, many Christians find themselves resorting to language that's been ingrained in them through a lifetime of church. Language they've learned in five-day clubs and youth groups and winter retreats. Language that gets fellow believers' heads nodding and everyone else's shaking in confusion. Language that means, essentially, nothing.

Here is a sample from a list that was put together by The North American Mission Board, ultimately to help its members avoid using churchspeak when talking with non-Christians. While I'm not sold on all the new terminology, I think (in general) it's helpful.

OLD	NEW
Born again, converted	Changed, transformed
Gospel	God loves us and sent His Son so that we can find forgiveness and a new life through Him
Have a burden	Be concerned
Salvation	Forgiven of wrongs and given eternal life
Sin, sinner	Acting against God's will and offending God's character
Testimony	Story

If you've ever talked about computers with an information technology person or listened as your doctor dictated your symptoms into his little recording device, you understand the plight of many non-Christians. You understand the blank stare as we tell them to "confess their sins and become born again, lest they face eternal damnation." *What?*

Over time, numerous versions of the Bible have been compiled to better speak to the people who are reading it, and (as Christians) it's important that we be intentional about doing the same. For me, the New Living Translation and The Message are wonderful examples of how Scripture can be stated in relevant, understandable ways, without altering the meaning of the original text.

Again, it's not about changing our *message*. It's about changing the *method* with which we share it.

12 Just Do It

Successfully Representing Jesus

Public and Relational

When Tiger Woods turned pro back in 1996, Nike instantly made him a rich man. Barely out of his teens, and not having won a single PGA tour event, Tiger was offered a five-year, $40 million contract.

Crazy, right?

Apparently not. Almost as quickly as it signed the deal, Nike was cashing in on their investment.

In 2001, the shoe company inked another five-year deal with Mr. Woods—this time for $100 million. Then, in 2006, Nike went even bigger—though the specifics were never disclosed.

Think about those numbers.

Essentially, Tiger got more than $20 million a year to have his picture taken and shoot a few TV commercials. Plus, he was loaded up with all the free products he could shoehorn into the trunk of his complimentary Buick. (Buick, American Express, Gillette, EA Sports, TAG Heuer, and Gatorade also each paid Woods millions to promote their brands.)

To be fair, Tiger got paid for more than a photo shoot every month or two. He got a seven-figure check because, as the face of Nike's golf division, Tiger Woods's name, image, and logo sold products. A lot. Nike sells golf balls, golf clubs, golf shoes, golf hats, and those infamous red golf shirts. They sell tees and towels and tan pants. Golf bags, golf gloves, and ball markers too. Even golf socks. That's right, socks!

But how?

How could one person's mere existence influence millions? How could one man's name alone impact people so strongly? How could one individual cause a significant portion of an entire generation to take notice?

Simply put, golfers wanted what Tiger had.

They wanted his skills, his swing, and his smile. They wanted his composure, his confidence, and his creativity. They wanted to walk to the first tee and hit a 300-yard drive as straight as an arrow. They wanted to effortlessly swing their way out of the deepest sand trap. They wanted to sink a 60-foot pressure putt on the eighteenth hole as the sun dipped behind the horizon. They wanted to pump their fist as the impossible happened.

They told themselves, *Tiger is the best golfer on the planet. Tiger uses Nike products. Therefore, if I use Nike products, then . . .*

From the moment he became a professional golfer, Tiger Woods was marketing gold. He not only energized people who already loved golf, but he also influenced nongolfers to try the sport. And try it with a brand-new sleeve of Nike golf balls.

When it comes to representing Jesus, are you and I doing that? Are we energizing people who already love Him, as well as influencing non-Christians to try Jesus? Do people really want what we have? Are we giving them a reason?

I'll say it again: Many people have no problem with Christ, but a big problem with Christians. Expressed in marketing terms, the product isn't the problem—the spokespeople are. Instead of bringing people to Jesus, it seems we're more effective at turning them away.

The word *Christian* means "little Christ." By definition, you and I are supposed to be the embodiment of Christ. Jesus with skin on. An earthly reflection of our Heavenly Father. Jesus' public relations team, so to speak.

For some reason, I'm not convinced that Christians truly understand what "public relations" really means. Many of us seem to choose only half of the term. We pick one word or the other. We opt to be public, but not relational—or we decide to be relational, but not public. Finding a balance between the two is apparently difficult.

Church isn't public. Sorry. Small group and Sunday school aren't public. AWANA and youth group aren't either. Neither is your Christian high school or college. None of them is bad, of course, but there is danger in fooling ourselves into thinking that our involvement in any of them constitutes publicly reaching out to our world for Christ.

Think about it this way: How much product would Nike sell if Tiger Woods holed himself up in a room full of Nike executives or other professional golfers all year? Wouldn't Nike be wasting money if their chief spokesperson never spoke with (or to) the company's potential customers?

On the flip side, preaching at people isn't relational. Sending chain e-mails asking friends and family to boycott certain companies isn't relational. Neither is chanting or holding up signs outside abortion clinics. It's not that there aren't times to stand up for what we believe. But if we think these things are effective ways to share Jesus with our culture—we're wrong.

Would people have gravitated to Nike if all their TV commercials featured Tiger berating Reebok or Titleist? If Mr. Woods did nothing to excite people about *his* product, but spent all his time ripping everybody else's golf equipment? Of course not.

Jesus, as always, is the perfect example. With ease, He walked the "public versus relational" tightrope. Jesus and the twelve disciples were a close-knit group of fellow believers, and they met with each other often. They "did life" together. But Jesus *also* spent much of his time interacting with Pharisees, tax collectors, and prostitutes. Jesus chastised, challenged, and condemned sin when it was appropriate. But He *also* lived, laughed, and loved on people, regardless of their background or lifestyle.

How much more effective might you and I become at representing Christ if we could also strike that balance?

How the Mighty Fall

On November 27, 2009, several large cracks began to form in Tiger Woods's story. In the course of twenty-four hours, Tiger went from being on *Sportscenter* to being on *Inside Edition*. He went from being on the cover of *Men's Health* to being on the cover of *National Enquirer*. He went from being a superstar to being a slimeball.

For more than a decade, much of the world saw Tiger as perfect. Not only was he was the best golfer on the planet, but he was (seemingly) a family man. He was a savvy entrepreneur and a philanthropist. He was good-looking and fabulously wealthy. But suddenly, in the course of a single news story, our perception of him began to change. We started to realize that what we *thought* Tiger was, wasn't at all what he *really* was.

I firmly believe that at least 90 percent of life's problems are a result of unmet expectations. We get the most frustrated, the most hurt, the most offended, when our theories don't live up to our realities. And that's exactly what happened with Tiger. Because of the picture Woods painted of himself, our society had high expectations for him, and ultimately those expectations were not met.

Few people would have been surprised (or would have cared) if the same thing had happened to Shaq or Eminem or Charlie Sheen. We don't expect a lot from them, so if something went wrong, nobody would be all that disappointed. Each has painted a very different picture of himself than Tiger did.

Christians who set themselves up as having all the answers—whether they are high profile or not—also risk Tiger-sized falls from grace. Jim Bakker, Jimmy Swaggart, and Ted Haggard come to mind. Both the Christian and non-Christian communities had lofty expectations for these men as authors, pastors, and denominational leaders, and each failed to meet those expectations. Like Tiger, they were *showing* one lifestyle and *hiding* another.

I'm not suggesting we set our standards so low that no one expects much of us. To me, it all comes back to telling an honest story. To living the same life in public as in private. To admitting our faults. To being forthright about what we struggle with. To letting people hold us accountable concerning our sinful tendencies.

Nobody is perfect, but plenty of us like to pretend we are. We share the good and hide the bad. We show the right and disguise the wrong. We talk the talk but don't walk the walk. Sadly, the longer we hide or disguise our sins, the more likely they are to become trends—then habits—then secondary lifestyles known to no one but ourselves. One-time mistakes (even for people in positions of influence) are easily forgiven. Lifelong trends are not.

Contrast the stories of Bakker, Swaggart, and Haggard—each of whom, apparently, struggled with hidden (and recurring) issues—with that of John Piper. In a 2010 letter posted to his *DesiringGod.com* website, the author, speaker, and pastor demonstrated the power of timely honesty. He wrote the following:

> I see several species of pride in my soul that, while they may not rise to the level of disqualifying me for ministry, grieve me, and have taken a toll on my relationship with Noël and others

who are dear to me. How do I apologize to you, not for a specific deed, but for ongoing character flaws, and their effects on everybody? I'll say it now, and no doubt will say it again, I'm sorry.

Shortly after writing this, Piper took an eight-month sabbatical from Bethlehem Baptist Church in Minneapolis. Despite requesting that the elders *not* pay him for his time away, they refused. The leadership of Bethlehem not only sent the Pipers a paycheck, but even appointed a group of men to hold Dr. Piper accountable while he was off. Though his words were appropriately vague, this church leader was up-front and honest *before* the fall. Before disturbing trends began to emerge. Before the issues he described took hold of his life. Before he was found out.

John Piper recognized and (most importantly) publicly acted on his humanness. No scandal. No church split. No breaking news stories. You and I might not be sports legends or spiritual leaders. But as we seek to represent Jesus to those around us, I think Piper sets a powerful example. Live an authentic life. Tell an honest story. Admit your daily struggles. Accept your obvious brokenness. Then commit to doing whatever it takes to become more like Christ.

Though it kind of sounds like it, the phrase "with great power comes great responsibility" is not from Proverbs. It's from Spider-Man. But just because this bit of wisdom originated in a comic book doesn't make it any less true. People in positions of authority *are* held to a higher standard—and their actions have greater consequences (both positive and negative) than those of people not in the public eye.

The Bible says the same thing in a different way: "Dear brothers and sisters, not many of you should become teachers in the church, for we who teach will be judged more strictly" (James 3:1).

Because of his public profile, Tiger Woods's actions hurt the organizations he represented. They hurt the PGA. They hurt Nike. They hurt the Tiger

Woods Foundation. They also hurt kids and families who looked up to him as a role model. Bakker, Swaggart, and Haggard had a similar ripple effect on their churches, communities, and even Christians in general. These men all found out the hard way that when power and influence are based on who you *say* you are, then it's only fair for them to be taken away based on who you *really* are.

The failure of a spokesperson *always* hurts the product, service, or cause that he or she represents. And the bigger the influence, the bigger the impact of the fall. No matter what your role in God's family, people are watching. Our daily actions affect others' perception of Jesus. We have a responsibility to—as closely as possible—make the lifestyle we *show* and the lifestyle we *live* actually match.

Math or Music

That's just a fantasy though, right? Since we're human, we can't possibly get our walk to live up to our talk, can we?

The simple answer is no.

While you and I are on lifelong journeys to become more and more like Jesus, we'll never fully make it. We're naturally hypocrites, and there's little we can do about it. Perfection is a goal, not a destination. We're going to fall. We're going to slip up. We're going to disappoint those who are watching how we live.

So how are we supposed to reconcile the idea of reflecting a perfect God with the knowledge that we're imperfect people? How can we take on the responsibility of representing Christ, with the guarantee that we're going to tarnish His image? How can we live up to our culture's expectations?

In a nutshell, the answer amounts to the difference between math and music.

Math is a science. It's a pass/fail thing. In general, there's one way to solve an equation, and the answer is either right or wrong. There is no in-between. Two plus two is always four. It's never three or five or seventeen. The hypotenuse of a triangle is always shorter than the length of the other two sides. The area of a rectangle is always length times width. Those equations never change.

When I was in elementary school, I loved math. Especially the timed tests. Our teacher would put fifty or one hundred simple problems on a sheet of paper, and the goal was to finish them as fast as you could. Not to brag, but I always finished first. And nearly every time, I got an A+.

In retrospect, my fast times and perfect scores fulfilled a need in me. Even at 6 or 7 years old, I liked knowing where I stood among my classmates. I liked putting my pencil down, looking around the room, and seeing everyone else still working. I liked getting my paper back from the teacher with a big, red 100 on the top, knowing that no one could possibly have beaten my score.

When perfection is possible, as it is in math, it allows us to rest. To stop working. To feel like we have mastered a discipline. To sit back and bask in the glow of being as good as we can possibly be.

Music, however, is different. It's an art. It's a process. In theory, there are an infinite number of ways to interpret any given song—and none of them is perfect. Some are better than others, but perfect? Not really. Technically, I could learn to play most of Jim Brickman's piano pieces exactly as he does, but the two of us will never be equals. There are probably thousands of cellists who can imitate Yo-Yo Ma, but their performances will never be comparable.

In high school marching band, we used to spend hours working on our marching technique, learning our places on the field, and memorizing our music. No matter how good we were as a group, we were never done. There were always steps to synchronize, positions to pinpoint, and rhythms to rehearse. Regardless of how hard we practiced, perfection was impossible; there was always room for improvement.

Taylor Swift sold more albums than any other artist in 2009—more than five million. At that point in her short career, the 19-year-old country star had already won multiple Grammys, American Music Awards, Academy of Country Music Awards, Country Music Awards, and one Video Music Award. When tickets for her 2010 Fearless tour went on sale, they sold out within minutes.

While most people are blown away by Taylor's live shows, like the rest of us, she's not perfect. In fact, after her 2010 Grammy Awards duet with Stevie Nicks, Miss Swift received some harsh reviews from music critics:

> Swift gave a strikingly bad vocal performance . . . sounding tinny and rhythmically flat-footed. —Ann Powers, *The Los Angeles Times*

> A night in the charmed life of Taylor Swift: Give an incredibly wretched vocal performance, go on to win the biggest Grammy of 2010 anyway. —Chris Richards, *The Washington Post*

Yet, despite the negative press, most of Taylor's fans (as well as the Grammy audience), loved her performance.

The CEO of Taylor's record label (Big Machine Records) is Scott Borchetta, and he understands why people gravitate to Swift's music, despite her imperfections. In a response to some of these reviews, Borchetta said that Taylor

> is the voice of this generation. She speaks directly to [her fans], and they speak directly back to her. This is about a true artist and writer and communicator. It's not about that technically perfect performance.

Though it's not necessarily a popular perspective, I try to think about the Christian life as if it was more music and less math. More grace and less law. Living by law encourages us to compare ourselves to other Christians.

Like the little first-grade me, looking around the room feeling good about myself for winning. Living by law allows us to feel like we've arrived. To get a superficial benefit for appearing perfect, like the Pharisees so often enjoyed.

Grace, however, puts everybody on a level playing field. We're all working toward the same goal, knowing that (on our own) none of us deserves heaven. There are no winners and no losers—just sinners, playing our music as best we can for a loving, compassionate Savior.

Whether you're a golfer or a gamer, a pastor or a plumber, an author or an architect, when it comes to living out your faith, there is no technically perfect performance. There is no 100. No A+. And because of that, there will always be a few critics.

If we as Christians are willing to show others our *true* selves, our humanness, our brokenness, then we'll consistently be living up to others' expectations—even when we fail. Christians will be seen as real people, not perfect people. As musicians, not mathematicians.

The good news is, if you're an authentic communicator (like Taylor Swift)—if you're open, honest, real, and raw—millions of people will resonate with your story anyway, flaws and all.

13 What If?

Radical Ways to Re-market Jesus

Green-Light Thinking

At the radio station where I work, we often engage in what's known as "green-light thinking." Essentially, green-light thinking is a brainstorming session where there are no bad ideas, and any problems, objections, or potential pitfalls of those ideas are tabled for another time. The goal is to get as many possibilities on the whiteboard as we can, hoping those possibilities will spur even more possibilities and eventually leave us with something pretty special.

Throughout history, countless people have turned entire industries on their heads with one simple (yet remarkable) idea. Someone came up with the idea to take the bags out of vacuum cleaners. Someone came up with the idea to put that yellow line across the football field during television broadcasts. Someone came up with the idea to use drywall instead of lathe and plaster. Someone came up with the idea to put pop-top lids on cans. Someone came up with the idea to put candy bar chunks in ice cream. (My wife would like me to publicly thank that person.)

When it comes to truly sharing Jesus with a consumer culture, I feel a little bit of green-light thinking is in order. As Christians, we've collectively avoided the remarkable because we're content with the ordinary, and we've allowed our habits and rituals to plow very narrow religious ruts.

In lieu of peppering this book full of answers, I've decided to put a few green-light ideas on the whiteboard. Ideas that might stretch your thinking. Ideas that might pull you out of your comfort zone. Ideas that might, at first, sound crazy, unnecessary, or even heretical. But they're just ideas. Consider them the start of a discussion.

Will they all work? Probably not. Will they all be effective? Not likely. Could one or two eventually lead to something pretty special—even revolutionary? With your personal vision and creativity, I think so. In fact, I hope you'll even add your own green-light ideas in the margins.

When putting *your* ideas on the whiteboard, let me encourage you to follow the advice of radio consultant Dan O'Day. In one of his training sessions, he suggested to the audience that we start with the impossible and work our way back to the just-barely-possible—rather than the other way around. Forget for a while about rules, history, financial constraints, and time barriers. If you can train your brain to think of the undoable first, it leaves a much greater likelihood that in the long run you will come up with something remarkable.

The Whiteboard

1. What if we spent a week with our family in Honduras or Haiti instead of Orlando or the Ozarks?

Is it possible to feel relaxed and refreshed after working in the sun, rather than lying under its rays? Which trip would be more memorable for our kids? Would they feel they missed out on something? Can we teach them it really is a small world after all without riding a ride?

Or what if, instead of taking one big vacation each year, we took two smaller ones? One family-focused. One others-focused. Just a couple of days working for a local ministry or a weekend serving in the inner city. How much good could we do?

2. What if we created our own, personal churches for the next month?

What if we invested our time for the next few weeks in being a part of *the* church without going to *a* church? How might we impact others around us without four walls and a stage and a coffee bar? Without three songs, a sermon, and an offering?

Maybe we could invite some friends to our home for dinner on Wednesday night or play golf with some guys from work on Sunday morning. Maybe we volunteer to serve at a soup kitchen or visit people in the hospital. Is there a nursing home nearby? Do the residents have someone come in to talk to them on Sunday mornings? Could you or I be that someone? What would it take to build solid relationships *outside* our comfortable Christian circles? What would it take to be "Jesus with skin on"? No agenda. No plan. Just love.

3. What if we paid for private school without sending our kids to one?

What if we enrolled our children at a state school or community college instead of a Christian university—and then used the money we saved to do something bigger than ourselves? Something God-sized? Something with eternal impact?

Over four years, the difference in college tuition could easily be $50,000. Probably more. That could pay for a lot of clean water in Africa. Or medicine in Haiti. It could buy a single mom a new minivan and pay off her credit card debt. It could start a scholarship fund for needy kids who want to take mission trips or go to camp. What if we got three or four other families to join us in our pledge? What kind of eternal projects could we collectively take on? Houses? Entire third-world villages?

4. What if we didn't write our tithe checks this week?

What if we instead gave the money to a single mom in our neighborhood or to the co-worker who just lost his job? What if we paid for a friend's child to go to basketball camp or to visit a parent who lives in another state? What if we bought dinner and took it to the couple down the street who is struggling with having sent their last child off to college?

Would we feel guilty? Would we be forsaking our respective churches? What does *tithe* really mean anyway? Does the Lord's work happen only on Sundays?

5. What if we went to the bar one Saturday night per month with our friends?

As Christians we frequently ask our friends, relatives, and co-workers to come with *us* to church, to vacation Bible School, to our Christmas musical, or Easter sunrise service. Places *we're* comfortable and *they're* not. Places *we* understand and *they* don't.

What if we spent more time on *their* turf—even if it meant periodically missing one of our customary Christian activities? Why not get uncomfortable for the sake of making a friend or deepening a relationship? Where do we think someone is more likely to open up and be real—at their hangout or ours?

6. What if we adopted a no-health-related-prayer-requests rule for a time?

Would our small group or Sunday school class survive without these sometimes superficial concerns? Would everybody just stare blankly if we couldn't ask them to pray for Great Aunt Edna's bunions or our nephew's cough? What if we eliminated prayer requests for safe travel too? Would there be anything left?

Taking this a step further, what if every prayer request had to be about *us*? About our struggles? About our sin? Could we be that honest? Could we trust the people around us enough to share those things? How might this simple exercise change our prayer lives?

7. What if we started Grubby Sunday at church?

What if we asked church members to show up looking like they were going to the grocery store, the post office, or the dog groomer? What if we removed the distraction of Sunday-only sport coats with ties for the men and dresses for the ladies once in a while and went to church "as is"? Pastors. Elders. Worship leaders. Everybody. (I know. It wouldn't be that hard for worship leaders.)

Could one simple change allow people to focus more on worship? To focus more on being real? To focus more on looking upward rather than outward? Isn't there some irony in singing "Come, Just As You Are," while wearing our Sunday best?

8. What if we joined (or started) the neighborhood poker game?

What if we could positively influence ten to twelve people every couple of weeks through a little Texas Hold 'Em? What if we even went so far as to personally provide the "pot" each week. Maybe an iTunes or Starbucks gift card? Maybe actual cash?

What kind of eternal impact might we have by starting or joining this kind of group? With whom in your subdivision could you start a relationship that you might not otherwise get the chance? (This same idea could apply for scrapbooking, fishing, motorcycling, quilting—you get the idea.)

9. What if we created a new line of Christian T-shirts?

What if we made these shirts just different enough to be conversation pieces, but not so different (featuring blood, nails, thorns) that they were off-putting? What if these shirts simply said "Loving" or "Joyful" or "Kind" on them? Would we be inspired to live up to what was on the front? Would others be inspired to ask us about them?

What about a shirt that said "I'm not just a sugarless nut in a world of Fruity Pebbles"? (See chapter 7.) Or had a giant less-than symbol on the front as a reminder of who Christ calls us to be?

10. What if we removed the signs in front of our church?

What if we made it *our* responsibility to tell people what was happening inside? What if we made it *our* job to bring nonbelievers through the doors? Would our attendance drop without service times or crosses or pithy sayings out front? Would anybody notice they were gone?

What if we challenged people at our church to personally be *living* signs for Christ? To take on the sole responsibility for growing the body, rather than counting on the sign or a yellow pages ad to do the job? Wouldn't those in our communities be more likely to visit when asked by a person rather than by a thing?

11. What if we chose not to pray before our meals or at bedtime?

How frequent would your prayer life be without those times? What if you never thanked God for your food or for the beautiful day? Would you have to rethink the contents of your regular prayers? Would they become more meaningful?

What if we set up entirely new prayer routines to get out of the rut so many of us are in? What about praying while we're in the shower or on our drive home from work? Why not pray while we wash the dishes or mow the lawn?

12. What if we chose to support the companies we believe in?

What if values-oriented and family-focused companies were inundated with positive letters (and financial support) from Christians? What if we told our friends about them? What if we joined fan pages on Facebook for these organizations and posted Twitter messages about them?

What if our voices (and money) were mysteriously absent from organizations that don't line up with our beliefs? If silence is deafening, what kind of impact could our absence have on R-rated movie makers, risqué clothing manufacturers, and shock-oriented TV advertisers? Would this be more effective than angry letters and boycotts?

13. What if we were intentional about befriending those people many Christians consider unlovely?

What if we built (appropriate) relationships with homosexuals, prostitutes, cross-dressers, and others we don't understand rather than mock or condemn them from a distance? What if we decided we were going to learn, firsthand, all we could about those we're ultimately trying to reach?

What are the chances that over time you and I would get a different opinion of some of these people? What are the chances that over time they would get a different opinion of us? How might those new opinions be virally spread throughout our respective communities?

14. What if our churches gave coffee and doughnuts to a shelter each week instead of to the congregation?

What if we asked people to bring a dish to share on Sunday, then boxed it all up and took it to a rescue mission? What if we committed to spending the money for weekly refreshments on stocking a local food pantry? What if we pledged that for every muffin we serve, for every cup of juice we hand out, we give the same number away?

Would people stop coming to services because they didn't get food? Have we been trained to be in fellowship only with coffee in our cups and muffins in our mouths?

15. What if we planned as many relationship-building times with friends, co-workers, and neighbors each week as church or small-group events?

What if we allotted time, money, and energy to putting our faith into action on a regular basis? What if we joined a bowling league or the PTA instead of a Thursday night Bible study? What if we coached our kid's soccer team instead of going to church on Wednesday?

How might we ensure we're actually playing the game and not just practicing for it? Are our weekly schedules so busy with church stuff that we don't have time to get out and touch people for Him? If we know what to do, are we leaving any room in our day to do what we know?

16. What if we gave up cable or internet access or a DVD club membership or a weekly latte so we could sponsor a child or buy supplies for a food pantry?

What if we started a Meals, Not Movies campaign in our hometowns where people give up one movie night a month and donate the saved money to a soup kitchen or a shelter? How many meals could $40 buy when you multiply it by a few hundred (or a few thousand) participants? What if you agreed as a family (or church or small group) that every time you went to Starbucks you would drop three dollars in a jar for the homeless?

What if we completely reevaluated our priorities as if looking through God's eyes? Is our *stuff* really that important? What kind of positive effect might purging it have on our families? On our communities?

17. What if we didn't read our Bibles every day?

What if we, instead, called and prayed with a friend? What if we mowed our next door neighbor's lawn? What if we mentored one day a week with our devotional time or wrote to our sponsored child during that half hour? What if we didn't check the little box next to our reading for the day?

Are we so bogged down in routine that we're not doing, we're just learning? Are we so dutiful that we're not passionate? Are we simply pacifying our own guilt with a ritual that doesn't actually benefit us?

18. What if we sold our church's building?

What if we rented a school, a movie theater, or a warehouse for services? What if we didn't have to mow the lawn, shovel the snow, pay the taxes, or replace the roof? Are there more efficient, more effective ways to use the money that comes in each week?

Would new people be more likely to walk through the doors of a school, a theater, or an empty warehouse? Might a multipurpose space be more usable for concerts, banquets, youth events, meetings, and other community outreach events than a single-use sanctuary?

19. What if we regularly met with atheists, agnostics, and people of non-Christian religions with the sole purpose of having them share their faith with us?

What if we had to do all the listening? What if we genuinely tried to understand where people of different faiths and backgrounds were coming from rather than condemn or chastise their lifestyle? (Notice I said "understand," not "accept" or "approve.")

Would we better relate to them in the long run? Would we better reflect Jesus? Didn't He model this idea for us in the Bible?

20. What if we frequently visited the churches of people who believe differently?

What if we took a Saturday night or Sunday morning to sit in a synagogue, a Kingdom Hall, a temple, or a Church of the Latter-day Saints? What kind of message might that send to the worshippers there? To other Christians?

Over time, would a Jehovah's Witness, Jew, or Mormon eventually be willing to visit your church? Could friendships be developed through this exercise? Could trust be built? Would stereotypes (on both sides) break down?

21. What if every church in America was open to the public seven days a week?

What if they offered basketball or karate or fitness classes? What if they built an indoor playground for moms and their kids? What if they set aside land for hiking or skating or running? What if they offered it all for free?

What if we used the church parking lot for Boy Scout car washes? What if we used the building for voter registration or MOPS (Mothers of Preschoolers) or city council meetings? What if we opened up the campus to the school district or chamber of commerce or business groups?

22. What if we decided to become homeless for a weekend?

What if we left home with nothing but the clothes on our backs and headed downtown? What if we devoted two full days to living with those who have nothing, and who are doing it right in our own community?

What might we learn about the men and women who live on the streets? How might we be able to impact their lives as one of them? Could we build a level of trust that would otherwise be impossible?

Conclusion
The End of the Beginning

One of my favorite catalogs came in the mail the other day. It was from Despair, Inc., the creator of the *Demotivator* posters. They are the glass-half-empty version of *Successories*. Perhaps the glass-all-empty version.

This off-the-wall company has created their own highly sarcastic versions of motivational posters, notepads, coffee mugs, and T-shirts.

One particular saying caught my attention. It read:

MARKETING:
Because making it look good now is more important
than providing adequate support later.

Absolutely hilarious. Mainly because it's so often true.

But in the context of this book, it's not funny at all.

While *Branded* has relied heavily on traditional marketing principles, it's critical that we not be so focused on attracting people to Jesus (marketing), that we leave them fending for themselves once they show up (customer support). Christianity already has too many customers and not enough marketers.

And as we've seen, mere customers aren't loyal. They only take and rarely give. They're not passionate about the brand. They can easily be talked into another product that on the surface looks like a better deal.

Getting people in the door of Christianity isn't good enough. Like Apple does so well, it's vital that Christian customers become followers. Followers become fans. And fans become marketers. That's the only way the cycle can continue. That's the only way Jesus won't get swallowed up in today's myriad of other options.

I've got to be honest: My conversations with Alan (my friend from the introduction) have gone nowhere. At least not yet. I've written a book on branding our Savior, yet I'm still faced with the same struggle as everyone else—trying to convince a culture that has no interest in Jesus that He's not only relevant to their lives, but necessary.

In one of our recent Facebook exchanges, Alan described how he thinks Christians view him and others like him:

> It seems most Christians can't grasp that some people believe religion to be complete and utter science fiction. Much like you might view Greek Mythology, Ghostbusters, Scientology, Spaceballs or Narnia.
>
> I also want people to know there are people who have well thought out reasons for not believing. Typically more thought out than those who believe in a god just because they've heard it from birth. There are millions of Americans who think as I do but aren't vocal about it. They attend church, they bow their heads when everybody else does, they say "thanks" when

somebody blesses them when they sneeze. It's going to be the next wave to "come out of the closet." Godless atheists, agnostics, humanists and free-thinkers aren't evil, they don't murder, they just don't subscribe to what boils down to be an imaginary friend. We aren't lost souls, we certainly don't worship a devil, and our values are plenty intact.

If that statement isn't reason enough to work harder at sharing Jesus with our culture, then I'm not sure what is. It's an uphill battle, but it's a battle worth fighting. For me, Alan has promised to read this book. That's all I can ask.

In a literary sense, this is the end. The end of the book. The end of the pep talk. But in a very real sense, it's only the beginning—a starting point. Given that we're living in the most spiritually competitive environment in history, there is much work to be done. It starts with you. And it starts with me.

Discussion Questions

Chapter 1.
Caught Off Guard: Why *Branded* Was Written

To read or reference:

> Later, Matthew invited Jesus and his disciples to his home as dinner guests, along with many tax collectors and other disreputable sinners. But when the Pharisees saw this, they asked his disciples, "Why does your teacher eat with such scum?" When Jesus heard this, he said, "Healthy people don't need a doctor—sick people do." Then he added, "Now go and learn the meaning of this Scripture: 'I want you to show mercy, not offer sacrifices.' For I have come to call not those who think they are righteous, but those who know they are sinners." (Matt. 9:10–13)

1. As Alan said, do you think Christians have more to learn from agnostics and atheists than they do from other believers? Why or why not?
2. How might interacting with people who don't believe as you do help sharpen your faith? How might it be a negative?
3. If we live in a culture that, for the most part, doesn't believe the Bible is the Word of God, how can we effectively show them and tell them about Jesus?

4. Are there any "checklists" or "playbooks" you have attempted to use to share Christ with someone? How well did they work—or not work?

5. What segment of our culture do you feel God has specifically gifted or positioned you to reach? How?

Chapter 2.
Putting Lipstick on a Pig: What Branding Jesus Is (and Isn't)

To read or reference:

> The end of the world is coming soon. Therefore, be earnest and disciplined in your prayers. Most important of all, continue to show deep love for each other, for love covers a multitude of sins. Cheerfully share your home with those who need a meal or a place to stay.
>
> God has given each of you a gift from his great variety of spiritual gifts. Use them well to serve one another. Do you have the gift of speaking? Then speak as though God himself were speaking through you. Do you have the gift of helping others? Do it with all the strength and energy that God supplies. Then everything you do will bring glory to God through Jesus Christ. (1 Peter 4:7–11)

> And then he told them, "Go into all the world and preach the Good News to everyone." (Mark 16:15)

1. In a general sense, do the words *marketing* or *branding* have negative connotations for you? Why or why not?

2. Have you ever been guilty of trying to share Jesus for the wrong reasons? What was your motivation and what was the result?

3. Which evangelism tactics do you need to change or do away with completely? Which new ones might be effective for you?

4. Describe a time when you have been turned off by another Christian's evangelism tactics?

5. How can you use your "paintbrush" (whatever the size) to affect the people around you?

Chapter 3.
Playing Monopoly by Yourself: What Branding Jesus Is Up Against

To read or reference:

> "Beware of false prophets who come disguised as harmless sheep but are really vicious wolves. You can identify them by their fruit, that is, by the way they act. Can you pick grapes from thornbushes, or figs from thistles? A good tree produces good fruit, and a bad tree produces bad fruit. A good tree can't produce bad fruit, and a bad tree can't produce good fruit. So every tree that does not produce good fruit is chopped down and thrown into the fire. Yes, just as you can identify a tree by its fruit, so you can identify people by their actions." (Matt. 7:15–20)

> "For false messiahs and false prophets will rise up and perform great signs and wonders so as to deceive, if possible, even God's chosen ones. See, I have warned you about this ahead of time." (Matt. 24:24–25)

1. Like Coke and Pepsi make each other better, who makes *you* better simply because they are around? Why do you think that is?
2. What ideas/beliefs/routines are competing with Christianity these days that weren't a generation ago?
3. What makes these other options so attractive to today's culture?
4. Research shows that fewer and fewer Americans are willing to commit to a specific faith. Why do you think that is?
5. What about Jesus is worthy of your undying allegiance? How can you express that to your friends and family who don't know Him?

Chapter 4.
I Wanted a Honda: How Branding Jesus Works

To read or reference:

> Jesus also taught: "Beware of these teachers of religious law! For they like to parade around in flowing robes and receive respectful greetings as they walk in the marketplaces. And how they love the seats of honor in the synagogues and the head table at banquets. Yet they shamelessly cheat widows out of their property and then pretend to be pious by making long prayers in public. Because of this, they will be more severely punished." (Mark 12:38–40)

1. Name one of your favorite products. Why is it a favorite? How does it meet your needs? Why do you have a favorable perception of it?
2. Are there any brands you have a negative perception of, even though you've never tried them? Why is that? Have you ever been pleasantly surprised by a product, despite your perception?
3. Why do you think many people today no longer feel they need Jesus? Or why is their perception of Christ so poor?
4. What are some ways we could change someone's perception of Christ? Have you ever seen it happen? Did it happen to you?
5. Are there things we do, rituals we go through, primarily for the approval of other Christians? How might we get better prepared for impacting people in the real world?

Chapter 5.
The Culture Club: Why Branding Jesus Is Difficult

To read or reference:

> When I was with the Jews, I lived like a Jew to bring the Jews to Christ. When I was with those who follow the Jewish law, I too lived under that law. Even though I am not subject to the law, I

did this so I could bring to Christ those who are under the law. When I am with the Gentiles who do not follow the Jewish law, I too live apart from that law so I can bring them to Christ. But I do not ignore the law of God; I obey the law of Christ. When I am with those who are weak, I share their weakness, for I want to bring the weak to Christ. Yes, I try to find common ground with everyone, doing everything I can to save some. (1 Cor. 9:20–22)

1. What is the predominant culture of the people you regularly associate with? (Is it racial, socioeconomic, religious, generational? Is it a combination?)
2. How has your culture shaped who you are, how you act, and what you believe? How might life be different if you were born into a different family or lived in a different place?
3. Why do so many Christians feel the need to change people's culture, rather than simply show them Jesus and let *Him* begin to change their heart?
4. How can you be intentional about reaching a specific culture (or segment of the population) to relate to them in a way they can identify with?
5. Knowing you can't possibly reach *everybody*, how might you become like Paul in 1 Corinthians 9 so you can reach *some*body?

Chapter 6.
The Product Isn't the Problem: Where Branding Jesus Has Gone Wrong

To read or reference:

> As he was speaking, the teachers of religious law and the Pharisees brought a woman who had been caught in the act of adultery. They put her in front of the crowd.
>
> "Teacher," they said to Jesus, "this woman was caught in the act of adultery. The law of Moses says to stone her. What do you say?"

They were trying to trap him into saying something they could use against him, but Jesus stooped down and wrote in the dust with his finger. They kept demanding an answer, so he stood up again and said, "All right, but let the one who has never sinned throw the first stone!" Then he stooped down again and wrote in the dust.

When the accusers heard this, they slipped away one by one, beginning with the oldest, until only Jesus was left in the middle of the crowd with the woman. Then Jesus stood up again and said to the woman, "Where are your accusers? Didn't even one of them condemn you?"

"No, Lord," she said.

And Jesus said, "Neither do I. Go and sin no more." (John 8:3–11)

"Do not judge others, and you will not be judged. For you will be treated as you treat others. The standard you use in judging is the standard by which you will be judged.

"And why worry about a speck in your friend's eye when you have a log in your own? How can you think of saying to your friend, 'Let me help you get rid of that speck in your eye,' when you can't see past the log in your own eye? Hypocrite! First get rid of the log in your own eye; then you will see well enough to deal with the speck in your friend's eye." (Matt. 7:1–5)

1. What celebrity do you most identify with? Why? Who can you not understand at all?
2. How does today's culture view Christians who "throw stones"? Why is that so easy for us to do?
3. In building relationships with non-Christians, what are some ways you can exceed their expectations *without* over-promising God?
4. What types of people do you try to avoid? What about them is such a turnoff?
5. Given the importance of your message, how can you effectively balance urgency and etiquette?

Chapter 7.
Spiritual Cereality: Why Branding Jesus Is Necessary

To read or reference:

> "I know all the things you do, that you are neither hot nor cold. I wish that you were one or the other! But since you are like lukewarm water, neither hot nor cold, I will spit you out of my mouth!" (Rev. 3:15–16)

> But there were also false prophets in Israel, just as there will be false teachers among you. They will cleverly teach destructive heresies and even deny the Master who bought them. In this way, they will bring sudden destruction on themselves. Many will follow their evil teaching and shameful immorality. And because of these teachers, the way of truth will be slandered. In their greed they will make up clever lies to get hold of your money. But God condemned them long ago, and their destruction will not be delayed. (2 Peter 2:1–3)

1. Mentally walk through the aisles of the grocery store or down the corridors at the mall. What products jump out at you? Which ones blend in? Why?
2. How do you think Jesus has gotten lost amid today's added spiritual competition? What happened?
3. How might we help Jesus stand out in a spiritually crowded marketplace without watering down the message or hiding what the Bible has to say?
4. What examples of "variety pack" faith have you seen? In the interest of tolerance, have we (as Christians) allowed this to happen?
5. If today's culture largely doesn't care one way or the other about Christ, how does that make our jobs more difficult? How do we begin to change that feeling? Is it possible?

Chapter 8.
Death of a Salesman: Effectively Advertising Jesus

To read or reference:

> Instead, you must worship Christ as Lord of your life. And if someone asks about your Christian hope, always be ready to explain it. But do this in a gentle and respectful way. (1 Peter 3:15–16)

1. Describe something that you know *how* to do but have never actually *done* in real life? Given the opportunity, do you think you could do it?
2. How does the relevance of something to your life affect your desire to learn or understand it? How can we use that principle to share Jesus more effectively?
3. Have you seen examples of the Circuit City–approach to evangelism? What about Best Buy's old tactics? How did the "customer" react to those approaches?
4. What can Christians learn from Best Buy in terms of adjusting to fit the needs of the culture? What specific changes do you think need to be made?
5. If you had to create a sixty-second Google commercial of your life, what would it say? Could you effectively share it with someone when given a chance?

Chapter 9.
Sweet Emotion: Honestly Sharing Jesus

To read or reference:

> Many years later, when Moses had grown up, he went out to visit his own people, the Hebrews, and he saw how hard they were forced to work. During his visit, he saw an Egyptian beating one of his fellow Hebrews. After looking in all directions to make sure no one was watching, Moses killed the Egyptian and hid the body in the sand. (Exod. 2:11–12)

Late one afternoon, after his midday rest, David got out of bed and was walking on the roof of the palace. As he looked out over the city, he noticed a woman of unusual beauty taking a bath. He sent someone to find out who she was, and he was told, "She is Bathsheba, the daughter of Eliam and the wife of Uriah the Hittite." Then David sent messengers to get her; and when she came to the palace, he slept with her. She had just completed the purification rites after having her menstrual period. Then she returned home. Later, when Bathsheba discovered that she was pregnant, she sent David a message, saying, "I'm pregnant." (2 Sam. 11:2–5)

1. What's your favorite book or movie? Why? What is it about the story that keeps you interested?
2. What makes *your* story interesting? What experiences have you had that a potential follower of Christ could relate to?
3. If talking only about Christianity's good stuff isn't believable, how do we find a successful balance when sharing the promises of God and the reality of our human situation? Is there one?
4. Has there been conflict in your story that you've intentionally kept hidden? How might sharing that conflict make your testimony more powerful?
5. Give an example of how one might try to *make* a friend or co-worker believe. Contrast that with things one might do to help a friend or co-worker *want* to believe.

Chapter 10.
White Headphones: Passionately Following Jesus

To read or reference:

> Three things will last forever—faith, hope, and love—and the greatest of these is love. (1 Cor. 13:13)

> "Your love for one another will prove to the world that you are my disciples." (John 13:35)

1. What makes Apple's products (iPod, iPhone, iPad) so appealing? Why are so many people compelled to tell others about them?
2. How do people see the love in your everyday life? What did you say or do today that could have (even unknowingly) shown someone else your spiritual set of white headphones?
3. What's your favorite recent television commercial? Why? Does it make you feel something (empathy, sadness, joy, hope)?
4. Name some of the emotions that Jesus makes you feel. What personal experiences might you share with a non-Christian about these feelings?
5. When sharing Jesus, how can we include both the *heart* and the *head*? How can we show Christ to be more than just words on a page?

Chapter 11.
Not Every Artist Wears a Funny Hat: Relevantly Showing Jesus

To read or reference:

Jesus said, "How can I describe the Kingdom of God? What story should I use to illustrate it? It is like a mustard seed planted in the ground. It is the smallest of all seeds, but it becomes the largest of all garden plants; it grows long branches, and birds can make nests in its shade." (Mark 4:30–32)

"If a man has a hundred sheep and one of them gets lost, what will he do? Won't he leave the ninety-nine others in the wilderness and go to search for the one that is lost until he finds it? And when he has found it, he will joyfully carry it home on his shoulders. When he arrives, he will call together his friends and neighbors, saying, 'Rejoice with me because I have found my lost sheep.' In the same way, there is more joy in heaven over one lost sinner who repents and returns to God than over ninety-nine others who are righteous and haven't strayed away!" (Luke 15:4–7)

1. Talk about a time you had *read* about something, but weren't truly touched by it until you *experienced* it for yourself.
2. Name some ways Christians have made Christ boring. What would you say to emphasize what makes Him so special?
3. Have you ever found yourself hiding behind a Christian symbol (necklace, bumper sticker, T-shirt)? Has it taken the place of actually engaging with people about your beliefs?
4. Think of a word or phrase you regularly use that has meaning within the Christian culture, but is unintelligible to those outside it. Why do you use it? How might you change it?
5. What Christian person, group, or organization do you see as doing an effective job reaching other Christians? What can you learn from those tactics?

Chapter 12.
Just Do It: Successfully Representing Jesus

To read or reference:

> Each time he said, "My grace is all you need. My power works best in weakness." So now I am glad to boast about my weaknesses, so that the power of Christ can work through me. That's why I take pleasure in my weaknesses, and in the insults, hardships, persecutions, and troubles that I suffer for Christ. For when I am weak, then I am strong. (2 Cor. 12:9–10)

1. Who is your favorite corporate spokesperson? Who is your least favorite? What about him or her makes the endorsement so effective (or ineffective)?
2. Have you ever had a public figure disappoint you? Who was it and why?
3. Do you struggle with matching the life you *show* and the life you *live*? Why is that so hard?
4. Who do you love despite their imperfections? Why? Do you feel *your* flaws somehow make you unlovable?

5. Are there battles you are fighting right now that you need to admit? Do you need accountability in some area of your life before a trend becomes a secondary lifestyle?

Chapter 13.
What If? Radical Ways to Re-market Jesus

To read or reference:

Looking at the man, Jesus felt genuine love for him. "There is still one thing you haven't done," he told him. "Go and sell all your possessions and give the money to the poor, and you will have treasure in heaven. Then come, follow me."

At this the man's face fell, and he went away sad, for he had many possessions. (Mark 10:21–22)

Remember this—a farmer who plants only a few seeds will get a small crop. But the one who plants generously will get a generous crop. You must each decide in your heart how much to give. And don't give reluctantly or in response to pressure. "For God loves a person who gives cheerfully." (2 Cor. 9:6–7)

At about that time Jesus was walking through some grainfields on the Sabbath. His disciples were hungry, so they began breaking off some heads of grain and eating them. But some Pharisees saw them do it and protested, "Look, your disciples are breaking the law by harvesting grain on the Sabbath."

Jesus said to them, "Haven't you read in the Scriptures what David did when he and his companions were hungry? He went into the house of God, and he and his companions broke the law by eating the sacred loaves of bread that only the priests are allowed to eat. And haven't you read in the law of Moses that the priests on duty in the Temple may work on the Sabbath? I tell you, there is one here who is even greater than the Temple! But you would not have condemned my innocent disciples if you knew the meaning of this Scripture: 'I want you to show mercy, not offer sacrifices.' For the Son of Man is Lord, even over the Sabbath!" (Matt. 12:1–8)

"The Son of Man, on the other hand, feasts and drinks, and you say, 'He's a glutton and a drunkard, and a friend of tax collectors and other sinners!' But wisdom is shown to be right by its results." (Matt. 11:19)

1. Are there any ideas in this chapter you think would be worth implementing in your own life? What would stop you from trying them?
2. Are there any ideas in this chapter you don't think would work at all? Why?
3. How are you already being radical in your community or neighborhood or workplace? What impact have you seen?
4. What radical ideas do you have to add to the list?
5. What outside obstacles or objections have the potential to get in the way of being radical? How can those be overcome?

Sources

Chapter 1: Caught Off Guard

14–15: *"Alan"*: Used by permission.

Chapter 2: Putting Lipstick on a Pig

17: *Merriam-Webster*: Merriam-Webster Online, s.v., "marketing," accessed December 2010, http://www.merriam-webster.com/dictionary/marketing.

23: *Gibbs*: Robert Gibbs cited by Stephanie Condon in "Pat Robertson Haiti Comments Spark Uproar," CBS News.com, Politcal Hotsheet, January 14, 2010, http://www.cbsnews.com/8301-503544_162-6096806-503544.html.

24: *Waters*: David Waters, "Haiti, the Devil and Pat Robertson," *Under God* (blog), *Washington Post*, January 13, 2010, http://newsweek.washingtonpost.com/onfaith/undergod/2010/01/haiti_the_devil_and_pat_roberton.html [*sic*].

24: *Raushenbush*: Paul Raushenbush, "Go to Hell, Pat Robertson: Haiti Needs

Help, Not Stupidity," blog, *The Huffington Post*, January 13, 2010, http://www.huffingtonpost.com/paul-raushenbush/go-to-hell-pat-robertson_b_422397.html.

Chapter 3: Playing Monopoly by Yourself

30: *World Christian Encyclopedia*: *World Christian Encyclopedia* cited by Bill Tenny-Brittian in *Hitchhiker's Guide to Evangelism* (St. Louis, MO: Chalice, 2008), 9.

30–32: *Pew Forum*: Pew Forum on Religion & Public Life, *U.S. Religious Landscape Survey*, "Summary of Key Findings," *Pew Forum on Religion & Public Life*, February 2008, http://religions.pewforum.org/reports.

Chapter 4: I Wanted a Honda

36: *Perception, by definition*: *Dictionary.com Unabridged*, s.v., "perception," accessed January 7, 2011, http://dictionary.reference.com/browse/perception.

37: *Consumer Reports* and *Edmunds*: See http://www.hyundaiusa.com/research-tools/reviews-awards.aspx.

38: *Consumer Reports*: "Don't Buy: Safety Risk—2010 Lexus GX 460," *ConsumerReports.org, Cars Blog*, April 13, 2010, http://blogs.consumerreports.org/cars/2010/04/consumer-reports-2010-lexus-gx-dont-buy-safety-risk.html.

38: *NHTSA*: Joseph B. White, "Why Toyota Rolled Over for Its SUVs," *WSJ.com*, The Wall Street Journal Digital Network, April 21, 2010, http://online.wsj.com/article/SB10001424052748703763904575196124098163614.html.

Chapter 6: The Product Isn't the Problem

58: *National Organization for Women*: Erin Matson, "Focus on the Family's Anti-Abortion Super Bowl Ad: Just Say No Thanks!" *Say It, Sister! NOW's Blog for Equality*, January 26, 2010, http://www.now.org/news/blogs/index.php/sayit/2010/01/26/focus-on-the-family -s-anti-abortion-super-bowl-ad-just-say-no-thanks.

Chapter 7: Spiritual Cereality

66: *Rutland*: Mark Rutland, *Behind the Glittering Mask* (Lakeland, FL: T.F.P., 1996), 95, 98.

Chapter 8: Death of a Salesman

76: *Google's 2010 Super Bowl spot*: You can currently view the ad at http://www.youtube.com/watch?v=nnsSUqgkDwU.

Chapter 9: Sweet Emotion

80: *Godin*: Seth Godin, *All Marketers Are Liars* (New York: Portfolio, 2005), 8–10.

Chapter 10: White Headphones

85: *less than 2 percent*: Arik Hesseldahl, "More People Use Apple Macs Than You Think," *MacDailyNews*, March 31, 2004, http://macdailynews. com/index.php/weblog/comments/more_people_use_apple_ macs_than_you_think_8_12_percent_of_homes_use_macs/.

85: *market cornered*: See chart 2 in John Thompson, "Computer Industry Sales Recovering, Jobs Flat," Federal Reserve Bank of Dallas, *Expand Your Insight*, June 11, 2003, http://wwwdallasfed.org/eyi/tech /0306computer.html.

86: *Fortune magazine*: Adam Lashinsky, "The Decade of Steve," *Fortune Magazine*, CNNMoney.com, November 5, 2009, http://money .cnn.com/2009/11/04/technology/steve_jobs_ceo_decade.fortune /index.htm.

86: *sixty-five billion dollars*: Peter Oppenheimer, United States Securities and Exchange Commission Form 10-K, Annual Report for Apple Inc. for fiscal year ended September 25, 2010, http://phx.corporate -ir.net/External.File?item=UGFyZW50SUQ9Njc1MzN8Q2hpbG RJRD0tMXxUeXBlPTM=&t=1.

86: *Godin*: Seth Godin, *Purple Cow* (New York: Portfolio, 2003), 31.

89: *Angelou*: Maya Angelou, Maya Angelou Facebook status update May 1, 2009, http://www.facebook.com/MayaAngelou?v=feed&story_ fbid=88309014336 (accessed January 11, 2011).

Chapter 11: Not Every Artist Wears a Funny Hat

93: *Downs*: Tim Downs, *Finding Common Ground: How to Communicate with Those Outside the Christian Community . . . While We Still Can* (Chicago: Moody Publishers, 1999), 55, 57.

98: *North American Mission Board*: "Unlearning the Lingo," *On Mission* online (July–August 2000), http://www.onmission.com/onmission pb.aspx?pageid=8589965509.

Chapter 12: Just Do It

103–4: *Piper*: John Piper, "John Piper's Upcoming Leave," Desiring God, March 28, 2010, http://www.desiringgod.org/resource-library /resources/john-pipers-upcoming-leave.

107: *Powers*: Ann Powers, "Ann Powers on the 2010 Grammy Awards: It's Not All About the Music," *Pop & Hiss* music blog, *Los Angeles*

Times, January 31, 2010, http://latimesblogs.latimes.com/music_
blog/2010/01/ann-powers-on-the-2010-grammy-awards.html.

107: *Richards*: Chris Richards, "Beyonce, Swift Score Big at the Grammys," *The
Washington Post* online, February 1, 2010, http://www.washington
post.com/wp-dyn/content/article/2010/01/31/AR2010013100757
.html.

107: *Borchetta*: Caitlin R. King, "Taylor Swift's Grammy Performance De-
fended by Her Label: 'Technical Issue,'" *The Huffington Post*, February 4, 2010, http://www.huffingtonpost.com/2010/02/04/taylor
-swifts-grammy-perf_n_448960.html.

Conclusion

120–21: *"Alan"*: Used by permission.

About the Author

Tim Sinclair is a husband to Heather, a father to Jeremiah and Elijah, and (for the past three years) a co-host to Pam on the duo's daily morning radio show. "Mornings with Tim and Pam" is heard by hundreds of thousands of people in Illinois and Indiana on Family Friendly WBGL, and the two have twice been nominated for "Air Personalities of the Year" at the ECHO Awards in Orlando, Florida.

Tim is a pastor's kid who briefly attended the University of Illinois before getting into radio and marketing full-time in 1998. Since then, he has helped write, voice, and produce commercials that have been heard on thousands of radio stations around the world. Some of his past clients include McDonald's, Word Records, Moody Publishers, and KSBJ/ Houston.

To connect with Tim: follow him on Twitter (@timjsinclair), like him on Facebook (www.facebook.com/timjsinclair), or visit his website (www.tim-sinclair.com).